DECENTRALIZED
SEARCH ENGINES
BY STEM SCHOOL

Decentralized Search Engines

How Blockchain & AI Are Revolutionizing the Web

By

STEM School

This Page Left Intentionally Blank

Contents

Introduction

The rise of decentralized search engines marks a significant evolution in how information is accessed, indexed, and presented on the internet. For decades, traditional search engines have operated under centralized models, where a few dominant companies have exercised disproportionate control over the flow of information. This centralization has given rise to numerous challenges, including privacy concerns, data monopolies, and algorithmic bias, all of which have far-reaching consequences for users and society at large. Decentralized search engines, powered by blockchain and artificial intelligence (AI), offer a compelling alternative that aims to create a more transparent, fair, and user-centric search ecosystem. This chapter explores the motivations behind the shift toward decentralization, the technological foundations that enable it, and the benefits it promises to deliver.

Limitations of Centralized Search Engines

Centralized search engines, such as Google and Bing, have long been the gatekeepers of information on the internet. Their algorithms determine which websites are ranked higher or lower in search results, influencing what information users are exposed to. While these platforms provide an essential service, their centralized nature introduces several significant limitations

Privacy Concerns

Centralized search engines collect and store vast amounts of user data, including search histories, browsing habits, and personal preferences. This data is often used to create detailed user profiles, which are then monetized through targeted advertising. While this model allows search engines to offer free services, it comes at the cost of user privacy. Personal data is stored on centralized servers, making it vulnerable to hacking, data breaches, and misuse. Furthermore, many search engines share user data with third-party advertisers and governments, raising concerns about surveillance and unauthorized access to personal information.

Data Monopolies

A handful of major companies dominate the search engine market, creating a data monopoly. Google, for example, holds more than 90% of the global search engine market share. This dominance gives these companies significant power over the internet ecosystem, including the ability to influence which websites receive traffic and which voices are amplified or suppressed. Data monopolies discourage competition and innovation, as smaller players lack access to the data and infrastructure needed to compete effectively.

Algorithmic Bias

Search engine algorithms are designed and controlled by centralized entities, making them susceptible to human bias and external influence. Algorithmic bias can manifest in the form of political favoritism, racial or gender discrimination, and economic bias. For example, search results can be manipulated to favor certain political ideologies or commercial interests, distorting the information landscape. Moreover, the algorithms are often opaque, meaning users have little understanding of how search results are ranked or why certain content appears more prominently.

Censorship and Content Control

Centralized search engines have the authority to censor content, either in response to government regulations or internal company policies. This has led to the suppression of certain viewpoints, the removal of controversial content, and the demonetization of independent creators. In politically sensitive regions, governments often pressure search engines to remove content critical of the ruling regime, leading to an erosion of free speech and open discourse.

Blockchain and AI in Decentralization

Decentralized search engines leverage blockchain technology and AI to address the shortcomings of centralized models. Blockchain provides a secure, transparent, and tamper-resistant ledger that records search activity and content indexing. AI enhances search accuracy and relevance by learning from user behavior without compromising privacy. The integration of these two technologies creates a decentralized search ecosystem where users retain control over their data and search results are determined by merit rather than corporate interests.

Blockchain Technology

Blockchain is a distributed ledger technology that records transactions across a network of computers in a secure and transparent manner. In the context of search engines, blockchain can be used to decentralize the indexing and ranking of search results. Instead of relying on a single company to control the search index, blockchain enables a peer-to-peer network where multiple nodes contribute to maintaining the index. This approach eliminates the possibility of single points of failure and ensures that search data is immutable and resistant to manipulation.

Blockchain also enhances transparency by allowing users to verify how search results are ranked and which sources are used. Smart contracts—self-executing contracts with terms written into code—can be used to automate the ranking process based on predefined rules and criteria. This ensures that search results are determined fairly and without bias. Additionally, blockchain allows users to control access to their data through encrypted keys, giving them the power to decide who can access their search history and personal information.

Feature	Centralized Search Engines	Decentralized Search Engines
Data Control	Controlled by the company	Controlled by the user through encryption and blockchain keys
Transparency	Opaque algorithms	Open-source and verifiable ranking algorithms
Security	Vulnerable to hacking and data breaches	Distributed and encrypted data storage
Monetization	Ad-based model reliant on personal data	User-controlled monetization through tokens and smart contracts
Bias	Subject to corporate and	Algorithmic fairness through community

Feature	Centralized Search Engines	Decentralized Search Engines
	political influence	governance

Artificial Intelligence

AI plays a crucial role in improving the relevance and accuracy of search results in decentralized models. Machine learning algorithms can analyze user behavior, search patterns, and contextual information to deliver highly relevant results without compromising user privacy. Unlike centralized models, where AI models are trained on aggregated user data stored in corporate servers, decentralized search engines use federated learning—a method that allows AI to learn from user data locally on the user's device without transmitting it to a central server.

AI-powered decentralized search engines can also combat algorithmic bias by relying on community-driven ranking models. Instead of a single entity defining the ranking criteria, decentralized AI models can be trained on diverse data sets contributed by the user community. This ensures that search results reflect a broader range of perspectives and are less prone to manipulation.

AI also enables personalized search experiences without invasive data collection. For example, natural language processing (NLP) models can understand the context and intent behind a search query, delivering more accurate and useful results. AI can also detect and filter out misinformation and low-quality content, improving the overall search experience.

Advantages of Decentralized Search Engines

Decentralized search engines offer several key advantages over their centralized counterparts

User-Controlled Data

In a decentralized model, users retain ownership of their data. Instead of storing search history and personal information on corporate servers, decentralized search engines store data on encrypted blockchain networks. Users can choose to share their data with specific services or keep it private, giving them greater control over their online footprint.

Reduced Censorship

Since decentralized search engines are governed by peer-to-peer networks rather than single entities, they are less susceptible to censorship and external influence. Content cannot be easily removed or manipulated, ensuring that users have access to a wider range of information.

Fairer Search Rankings

Decentralized search engines use transparent and open-source ranking algorithms, reducing the potential for manipulation and bias. Search results are ranked based on merit and relevance rather than corporate interests or advertising revenue.

Improved Search Accuracy Through AI

AI models in decentralized search engines learn from user interactions while preserving privacy. Machine learning algorithms can deliver highly relevant search results by understanding the intent and context behind user queries. AI-driven ranking models are also more adaptable, capable of evolving based on real-time user feedback.

Token-Based Incentives

Blockchain-based search engines can introduce token-based incentives to reward users for contributing data, verifying content, or improving search algorithms. Users can earn tokens for participating in the ecosystem, creating a self-sustaining and user-driven search model.

The combination of blockchain and AI holds the potential to transform the search engine landscape by creating a more transparent, fair, and privacy-respecting model. The following chapters will explore the technical architecture of decentralized search engines, the challenges involved in building and scaling them, and the potential impact on the future of information access and digital privacy.

Chapter 1

Evolution of Search Engines and the Rise of Decentralization

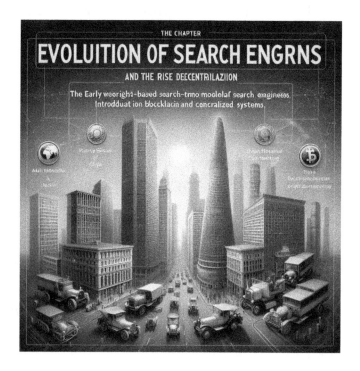

The evolution of search engines has fundamentally shaped how information is accessed and consumed in the digital age. From the early days of basic keyword-based search models to the sophisticated AI-driven algorithms used by modern search engines, the ability to retrieve and organize information has become one of the most influential technological advancements of the internet era. However, the dominance of a few centralized search engine providers has introduced significant concerns related to privacy, data exploitation, and the monopolization of information access. The rise of blockchain and decentralized protocols in the web ecosystem is now paving the way for a new era of decentralized search engines. This chapter explores the historical development of search engines, the challenges posed by centralized models, and the growing need for a decentralized alternative that prioritizes user privacy and data control.

Early Search Engines

In the early days of the internet, information retrieval was highly unorganized and fragmented. Early search engines operated as manual directories rather than automated indexing systems. Websites were cataloged manually, and users had to browse through hierarchical directories to find information. Some of the first recognizable search engines included Archie (1990), which indexed FTP archives, and Veronica

(1992), which provided keyword-based searching of Gopher directories. These early systems were limited in scope and could only search a small portion of the growing web.

The launch of WebCrawler in 1994 marked the transition toward automated indexing and keyword-based search. WebCrawler was the first search engine to index the full text of web pages, allowing users to search for specific terms rather than relying on predefined categories. This innovation significantly improved the efficiency and accuracy of search results. By the mid-1990s, other search engines such as AltaVista, Excite, and Lycos emerged, each introducing new methods for crawling and ranking web pages.

The major turning point came with the introduction of Google's PageRank algorithm in 1998. PageRank revolutionized search by ranking web pages based on the number and quality of links pointing to them. This approach provided more relevant and reliable search results, quickly making Google the dominant search engine. Google's algorithm leveraged a combination of link analysis, content matching, and user behavior to continuously refine search rankings, setting the foundation for modern search models.

Early Search Engines	Year Introduced	Key Innovation

Early Search Engines	Year Introduced	Key Innovation
Archie	1990	Indexed FTP archives
Veronica	1992	Keyword-based search for Gopher directories
WebCrawler	1994	First full-text indexing search engine
AltaVista	1995	Early natural language processing for search queries
Google	1998	PageRank algorithm based on link authority

Dominance of Centralized Search Engines

By the early 2000s, Google emerged as the dominant search engine, overtaking competitors through its highly efficient indexing, fast query response times, and increasingly accurate search results. Microsoft's Bing entered the market in 2009, but despite aggressive competition, Google retained a commanding market share. As of 2025, Google accounts for over 90% of the global search engine market share, with Bing holding a distant second place at around 3%. This dominance has positioned Google as the de facto gateway to the internet, giving the company enormous control over the flow of information.

The centralized nature of these search engines means that a small number of corporations have near-total control over how information is ranked, indexed, and monetized. The algorithms used to rank search results are proprietary and opaque, making it difficult for users to understand why certain websites are ranked higher than others. The reliance on advertising as the primary revenue model has further skewed search rankings, as paid advertisements and sponsored content often receive priority placement. This has created an ecosystem where search engines are incentivized to prioritize corporate interests over user relevance and fairness.

Privacy Issues and Data Exploitation

The dominance of centralized search engines has given rise to significant privacy concerns and data exploitation. Google and Bing collect vast amounts of user data, including search history, location data, browsing behavior, and personal preferences. This data is aggregated and used to create detailed user profiles, which are then sold to advertisers for targeted marketing.

The use of personal data to deliver personalized search results and advertisements creates a fundamental

19

conflict of interest. While personalized results may improve search relevance, they also expose users to algorithmic echo chambers, where information is filtered and presented based on past behavior rather than objective relevance. This reduces the diversity of information and reinforces existing biases.

Moreover, the storage of personal data on centralized servers creates a single point of vulnerability. High-profile data breaches at companies like Google and Yahoo have exposed the personal information of billions of users, highlighting the inherent security risks of centralized data storage. Governments and law enforcement agencies have also gained access to search engine data through legal orders and surveillance programs, further compromising user privacy.

Issue	Centralized Search Engines
Data Collection	Extensive collection of personal data and search history
User Privacy	User profiles shared with advertisers and third parties
Security	Centralized servers vulnerable to hacking and data breaches
Algorithmic	Filter bubbles and reinforcement of user

Issue	Centralized Search Engines
Bias	biases
Transparency	Proprietary algorithms with no user insight into ranking methods

Blockchain and Decentralized Protocols

The rise of blockchain technology and decentralized web protocols (often referred to as Web3) is now challenging the dominance of centralized search engines. Blockchain provides a secure, transparent, and immutable ledger that records data across a distributed network. This decentralized model removes the need for a central authority, allowing users to interact directly with search infrastructure without relying on a corporate intermediary.

In a blockchain-based search engine, indexing and ranking data are stored on a decentralized network of nodes rather than a central server. Each node contributes to maintaining the search index and verifying the accuracy of search results. This model ensures that no single entity has control over the search algorithm or data, reducing the risk of manipulation and censorship. Blockchain also enables users to control access to their personal data through encryption keys, ensuring that data remains private and secure.

Smart contracts—self-executing contracts stored on the blockchain—can automate the ranking and reward systems within a decentralized search engine. For example, users could earn tokens for contributing to the search network or verifying search results, creating an incentive-based model where users benefit directly from their participation.

Feature	Centralized Search Engines	Decentralized Search Engines
Data Storage	Centralized servers	Distributed blockchain network
User Privacy	Controlled by the company	Controlled by the user through encryption
Algorithm Transparency	Proprietary and hidden	Open-source and verifiable
Monetization	Advertising-driven	Token-based user incentives
Security	Vulnerable to breaches	Resistant to hacking through decentralization

The Need for a Decentralized Search Model

The increasing concentration of power in the hands of a few dominant search engine providers has created a growing demand for an alternative model that prioritizes user privacy and data sovereignty. A decentralized search engine addresses the fundamental flaws of the centralized model by distributing control over indexing, ranking, and data storage across a network rather than relying on a single corporation.

Decentralization enhances user privacy by eliminating the need for data collection and targeted advertising. Instead of building user profiles to serve ads, decentralized search engines can rely on blockchain-based incentives to reward user participation and content verification. Transparency is also improved, as search algorithms are stored on a public blockchain where users can verify the ranking criteria and ensure that search results are determined fairly.

The combination of blockchain and AI presents a powerful opportunity to create a search engine that is not only more secure and private but also more accurate and unbiased. AI-driven ranking models can adapt to user behavior while preserving privacy through federated learning and encrypted data processing. Blockchain ensures that the data used to train these models remains secure and tamper-proof, creating a search ecosystem that is resistant to manipulation and bias.

The shift toward decentralized search represents more than just a technological evolution—it is a fundamental shift in the balance of power between corporations and users. By reclaiming control over personal data and search relevance, users can create a more open, transparent, and equitable information ecosystem.

Chapter 2

Fundamentals of Search Engine Architecture

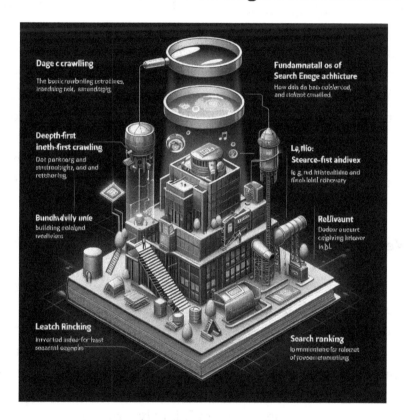

Search engines are complex systems designed to collect, organize, and retrieve information from the vast expanse of the internet. The fundamental architecture of a search engine consists of several key components, including data collection through web crawling, data parsing and structuring, indexing, and search ranking based on relevance and authority. Understanding how these components work together is essential for building an efficient and scalable search engine. This chapter will explore the inner workings of search engines, including web crawling strategies, data parsing using HTML and XML, inverted index construction, and search ranking models. It will also provide practical examples using Python and Elasticsearch to demonstrate the technical implementation of these components.

Web Crawling Strategies

Web crawling is the first step in the search engine process, where automated programs known as crawlers or spiders systematically browse the internet to collect data from web pages. Crawlers follow links from one page to another, collecting HTML content, metadata, and other structured data. The challenge in web crawling lies in efficiently discovering and processing large volumes of web pages while avoiding overloading websites or violating the rules defined in the robots.txt file.

Two primary strategies for web crawling are depth-first search (DFS) and breadth-first search (BFS).

Depth-First Search (DFS) Crawling

In depth-first search crawling, the crawler follows a single path through the link structure of a website until it reaches the deepest possible node before backtracking to explore other links. This strategy allows the crawler to thoroughly explore individual websites but can lead to poor coverage if the crawler gets trapped in long chains of links.

The depth-first search crawling strategy is implemented using a stack-based approach. The crawler pushes newly discovered links onto the stack and continues down the current path until no more links are available, at which point it backtracks and explores the next available link.

Breadth-First Search (BFS) Crawling

In breadth-first search crawling, the crawler explores all the links at the current level of depth before moving to the next level. This strategy ensures a wider and more balanced coverage of the web, as the crawler systematically expands the search area rather than getting stuck in deep link chains. BFS is implemented using a queue-based approach, where newly discovered links are added to the queue, and the crawler processes them in the order they were discovered.

The choice between DFS and BFS depends on the desired search depth and the nature of the data being collected. BFS is generally preferred for search engines because it ensures more comprehensive coverage and reduces the risk of missing important pages. However, DFS may be more suitable for targeted crawling when the goal is to exhaustively explore a specific domain.

The following table summarizes the differences between DFS and BFS crawling

Strategy	Method	Pros	Cons
Depth-First Search (DFS)	Stack-based	Efficient for deep exploration of specific sites	May miss broad coverage of the web
Breadth-First Search (BFS)	Queue-based	Provides balanced coverage and avoids getting stuck in loops	Slower for deep exploration

Python Implementation of BFS Crawling

The following Python code demonstrates a basic BFS crawling strategy using the requests and BeautifulSoup libraries to extract links and content from web pages

28

```python
import requests
from bs4 import BeautifulSoup
from collections import deque

def bfs_crawler(start_url, max_pages)
    visited = set()
    queue = deque([start_url])

    while queue and len(visited) < max_pages
        url = queue.popleft()
        if url not in visited
            try
                response = requests.get(url)
                soup = BeautifulSoup(response.content, 'html.parser')
                print(f'Crawling  {url}")

                for link in soup.find_all('a', href=True)
                    next_link = link['href']
                    if next_link.startswith('http')  and  next_link  not  in
visited
                        queue.append(next_link)

                visited.add(url)
            except Exception as e
                print(f'Failed to crawl {url}  {e}")

bfs_crawler('https //example.com', 10)
```

This example implements a BFS crawler that starts with a seed URL and explores linked pages, adding new links to the queue and processing them in the order they were discovered.

Data Parsing and Structuring Using HTML

Once a web page has been crawled, the next step is parsing the content and structuring it for indexing. Web pages are primarily written in HTML (HyperText Markup Language), which defines the structure and content of the page using a tree-based format of nested elements. XML (eXtensible Markup Language) is also used for structured data representation in web services and RSS feeds.

HTML parsing involves extracting the text content, metadata, links, and media elements from the document. The BeautifulSoup library in Python provides an efficient way to parse and extract information from HTML documents. XML parsing follows a similar process but requires additional handling for namespaces and structured data.

Python Implementation of HTML Parsing

The following Python code demonstrates how to parse HTML content using BeautifulSoup to extract the title, headings, and links from a web page

```
from bs4 import BeautifulSoup
import requests

url = 'https //example.com'
response = requests.get(url)
soup = BeautifulSoup(response.content, 'html.parser')
```

```
title = soup.title.string
headings = [h.get_text() for h in soup.find_all('h1')]
links = [a['href'] for a in soup.find_all('a', href=True)]

print(f"Title {title}")
print(f"Headings {headings}")
print(f"Links {links}")
```

This example extracts and displays the title, headings, and links from the HTML document, allowing structured data to be generated for indexing.

Building and Maintaining an Inverted Index

An inverted index is the core data structure used in search engines to enable fast text search. An inverted index maps words (or tokens) to the list of documents and positions where they appear. This allows the search engine to quickly identify which documents contain a given search term and compute the relevance of each result.

The inverted index is built by tokenizing the text content into individual terms, normalizing them (e.g., converting to lowercase, removing punctuation), and storing the document ID and term position in a searchable index.

The following table demonstrates the structure of an inverted index for three example documents

Term	Document IDs	Positions
"search"	[1, 2, 3]	[5, 12, 3]
"engine"	[1, 2]	[6, 14]
"data"	[2, 3]	[7, 4]

Python Implementation of an Inverted Index

```
from collections import defaultdict

def build_inverted_index(docs)
    index = defaultdict(list)
    for doc_id, doc in enumerate(docs)
        words = doc.lower().split()
        for position, word in enumerate(words)
            index[word].append((doc_id, position))
    return index

docs = ["Search engines use data to rank results",
        "Data science is the backbone of search engines",
        "Efficient search is based on fast indexing"]

inverted_index = build_inverted_index(docs)
print(inverted_index)
```

Search Ranking Based on Relevance

Modern search engines use a combination of relevance and link authority to rank search results. Relevance is computed using term frequency-inverse document frequency (TF-IDF), which measures how often a term appears in a document relative to its frequency across the entire document set. Link authority is measured using algorithms like PageRank, which rank pages based on the number and quality of inbound links.

The following formula defines TF-IDF

TF-IDF=Term Frequency×log Total Number of DocumentsNumber of Documents Containing the Term\text{TF-IDF} = \text{Term Frequency} \times \log \frac{\text{Total Number of Documents}}{\text{Number of Documents Containing the Term}}TF-IDF=Term Frequency×logNumber of Documents Containing the TermTotal Number of Documents

Combining TF-IDF with PageRank allows the search engine to rank pages based on both content relevance and web authority, producing more accurate and trustworthy search results.

Chapter 3

Introduction to Blockchain Technology

Blockchain technology has emerged as a revolutionary method for securing and decentralizing data. At its core, blockchain is a distributed ledger that records transactions in a secure, immutable, and transparent manner. Unlike traditional databases controlled by centralized authorities, a blockchain is maintained by a network of independent nodes that work together to validate and record transactions without the need for a central entity. This decentralized nature makes blockchain highly resistant to fraud, censorship, and single points of failure, making it a perfect foundation for building decentralized search engines.

In the context of search engines, blockchain technology addresses some of the major challenges posed by centralized models, such as data manipulation, biased ranking, and user privacy violations. By decentralizing data storage and using cryptographic techniques to secure data, blockchain enables a more transparent, secure, and unbiased search engine architecture. This chapter will explore the fundamental components of blockchain technology, including blockchain data structures, consensus mechanisms, smart contracts, and decentralized data handling using the InterPlanetary File System (IPFS). Practical examples and code snippets using Ethereum and Solidity will be provided to help readers understand how to implement blockchain-based search engines.

Blockchain Data Structures

A blockchain is essentially a chain of blocks that store transaction data in a secure and immutable manner. Each block contains a set of data, a cryptographic hash of the previous block, a timestamp, and a unique identifier. This creates a linked structure where each block depends on the integrity of the previous one, forming a secure and verifiable chain. The primary components of a blockchain data structure are

Block A block is the basic unit of data storage in a blockchain. Each block contains a collection of transactions, a unique block hash, the hash of the previous block, and a timestamp.

Merkle Tree A Merkle tree is a data structure used to efficiently verify the integrity of large datasets. In a Merkle tree, data is grouped into pairs, and each pair is hashed together until a single root hash (the Merkle root) is generated. The Merkle root is stored in the block header and serves as a fingerprint of all transactions in the block.

Cryptographic Hashing Blockchain security relies on cryptographic hashing, which converts data into a fixed-length string (the hash). Any change in the input data will produce a completely different hash, making it impossible to alter the data without invalidating the entire chain.

The Merkle tree structure is represented as follows

```
    Root Hash
     /    \
  Hash1    Hash2
  /  \    /  \
Tx1 Tx2 Tx3 Tx4
```

This structure allows efficient verification of data integrity. For example, to prove that Tx1 is part of the blockchain, the hash path from Tx1 to the root hash can be computed and verified without needing to store all transaction data.

Consensus Mechanisms

Consensus mechanisms are protocols used by blockchain networks to achieve agreement on the state of the ledger among distributed nodes. Since blockchain is decentralized, there is no central authority to validate transactions, so consensus mechanisms enable the network to agree on which transactions are valid and should be added to the blockchain. The most commonly used consensus mechanisms are Proof of Work (PoW), Proof of Stake (PoS), and Proof of Authority (PoA).

Proof of Work (PoW)

Proof of Work is the consensus mechanism used by Bitcoin and several other blockchains. In PoW, nodes (called miners) compete to solve complex mathematical puzzles. The first miner to solve the puzzle gets the right to add the next block to the blockchain and is rewarded with newly minted cryptocurrency and transaction fees. The computational difficulty ensures that it is extremely difficult for any single entity to manipulate the blockchain.

The following Python code snippet demonstrates a simplified PoW implementation

```
import hashlib
import time

def proof_of_work(last_proof)
    proof = 0
    while  hashlib.sha256(f'{last_proof}{proof}'.encode()).hexdigest()[
4] != "0000"
        proof += 1
    return proof

last_proof = 100
start_time = time.time()
new_proof = proof_of_work(last_proof)
end_time = time.time()

print(f'Proof found   {new_proof} in {end_time - start_time}
seconds")
```

Proof of Stake (PoS)

In Proof of Stake, validators are chosen based on the amount of cryptocurrency they hold and are willing to "stake" as collateral. The probability of being selected as the next block validator increases with the size of the stake. PoS is more energy-efficient than PoW because it does not require intensive computational work.

Proof of Authority (PoA)

Proof of Authority is a consensus mechanism where a limited number of trusted nodes (authorities) are responsible for validating transactions. PoA is highly efficient and suitable for private or permissioned blockchains where trust among validators is established beforehand.

The following table compares the three consensus mechanisms

Consensus Mechanism	Strengths	Weaknesses	Use Cases
Proof of Work (PoW)	Highly secure, resistant to attacks	High energy consumption	Bitcoin, Ethereum (before transition to PoS)
Proof of Stake (PoS)	Energy-efficient, fast	Centralization risk due to large stakes	Ethereum, Cardano, Polkadot

Consensus Mechanism	Strengths	Weaknesses	Use Cases
Proof of Authority (PoA)	Fast, low resource requirements	Centralized trust	Private blockchains

Smart Contracts Applications (DApps)

Smart contracts are self-executing contracts written in code that automatically enforce the terms and conditions agreed upon by the parties involved. They are deployed on the blockchain and run independently without human intervention. Smart contracts enable the creation of decentralized applications (DApps) that operate transparently and securely on blockchain networks.

The following Solidity code defines a simple smart contract on Ethereum

```
pragma solidity ^0.8.0;

contract SimpleContract {
    string public message;

    constructor(string memory _message) {
        message = _message;
    }
```

```
function updateMessage(string memory _newMessage) public {
    message = _newMessage;
}
}
```

In this example, the smart contract stores a message that can be updated using the updateMessage function. The contract is deployed on the Ethereum network, where transactions are secured using blockchain.

Handling Blockchain Data Using IPFS

The InterPlanetary File System (IPFS) is a decentralized protocol for storing and sharing files in a distributed network. Unlike traditional storage systems where files are stored in centralized servers, IPFS uses a peer-to-peer network where files are broken into chunks, cryptographically hashed, and stored across multiple nodes.

IPFS generates a unique content identifier (CID) for each file, which can be used to retrieve the file from the network. This enables decentralized search engines to store and retrieve indexed data securely and efficiently.

The following command uploads a file to IPFS

ipfs add filename.txt

The CID generated can be used to retrieve the file

```
ipfs cat <CID>
```

By combining blockchain and IPFS, decentralized search engines can securely store data, ensure data integrity, and enable fast retrieval without relying on centralized storage solutions.

Chapter 4

Designing a Blockchain-Based Search Infrastructure

Designing a blockchain-based search infrastructure involves creating a decentralized architecture where data storage, indexing, and query processing occur without relying on a central authority. Unlike traditional search engines, which are controlled by large corporations and rely on centralized servers for data storage and processing, a blockchain-based search engine distributes these tasks across a network of independent nodes. This decentralized model ensures that data integrity, security, and transparency are maintained while also protecting user privacy and eliminating the risks of single points of failure and data manipulation.

The core components of a blockchain-based search infrastructure include a peer-to-peer (P2P) network for data exchange, decentralized data storage using the InterPlanetary File System (IPFS), smart contracts for handling query processing and result ranking, and a token-based incentive system to reward participants who contribute to crawling and indexing. This chapter will explore each of these components in detail, providing sample implementations using Solidity, IPFS, and Go-Ethereum to help readers understand how to construct a functioning decentralized search engine.

Setting Up a Peer-to-Peer (P2P) Network

A peer-to-peer (P2P) network forms the foundation of a decentralized search engine. In a P2P network, nodes communicate directly with each other rather than relying on a central server. Each node in the network acts as both a client and a server, meaning that it can request data from other nodes and also provide data to others. This creates a distributed environment where data is exchanged and stored in a decentralized manner, enhancing security and reducing the risk of censorship or data manipulation.

To set up a P2P network, each node must maintain a list of neighboring nodes, establish secure communication channels, and implement a protocol for exchanging data. The most commonly used protocols for P2P communication include the BitTorrent protocol, the Kademlia distributed hash table (DHT), and libp2p (used in IPFS).

The following diagram illustrates the structure of a P2P network

Each node in the P2P network is identified by a unique public key and communicates using encrypted channels. When a new node joins the network, it uses a bootstrapping process to discover neighboring nodes and establish connections. Nodes also use a gossip protocol to share information about network changes, such as new nodes joining or existing nodes going offline.

The following Go code snippet demonstrates a simple implementation of a P2P node using the libp2p library

```go
package main

import (
        "fmt"
```

```
        "log"
        "context"
        "github.com/libp2p/go-libp2p"
)

func main() {
        host, err  = libp2p.New()
        if err != nil {
                log.Fatal(err)
        }
        fmt.Println("P2P node started with ID ", host.ID())
        select {} // Keep the program running
}
```

In this example, the node is initialized using the libp2p.New() function, which automatically creates a unique peer ID and sets up secure communication channels. The node will remain active and listen for incoming connections until terminated.

IPFS to Store and Retrieve Indexed Data

The InterPlanetary File System (IPFS) is a distributed file storage system that allows data to be stored and retrieved in a decentralized manner. In a blockchain-based search engine, IPFS is used to store indexed data, such as web pages, metadata, and search results. Instead of storing files in a single location, IPFS breaks them into smaller chunks, assigns each chunk a unique content identifier (CID), and distributes them across the network.

When a file is uploaded to IPFS, the CID is computed using a cryptographic hash of the file's contents. This ensures that files with identical content produce the same CID, enabling deduplication and efficient data retrieval. The CID acts as a permanent reference to the file and allows the file to be retrieved from any node that has a copy.

To store data on IPFS, the following command can be used

ipfs add file.txt

The output will display the CID

QmZ7......2f8 (CID)

To retrieve the file, the CID is passed to the ipfs cat command

ipfs cat QmZ7......2f8

By storing indexed data in IPFS, decentralized search engines can ensure that data is immutable, secure, and highly available even if individual nodes go offline.

Smart Contracts for Query Processing

Smart contracts are self-executing programs deployed on a blockchain that automate the execution of predefined actions when specific conditions are met. In a decentralized search engine, smart contracts can be used to handle query processing and result ranking in a transparent and tamper-proof manner.

A search query can be processed using a smart contract that retrieves the relevant data from IPFS, ranks the results based on a predefined algorithm, and returns the top-ranked results to the user. The ranking algorithm can be based on factors such as keyword relevance, user feedback, and the reputation of the data source.

The following Solidity code snippet demonstrates a basic smart contract for handling search queries

```solidity
pragma solidity ^0.8.0;

contract SearchEngine {
    struct Result {
        string data;
        uint score;
    }

    mapping(string => Result[]) public results;

    function addResult(string memory query, string memory data, uint score) public {
        results[query].push(Result(data, score));
    }

    function getTopResult(string memory query) public view returns (string memory) {
```

```
    uint highestScore = 0;
    string memory bestResult;

    for (uint i = 0; i < results[query].length; i++) {
        if (results[query][i].score > highestScore) {
            highestScore = results[query][i].score;
            bestResult = results[query][i].data;
        }
    }

    return bestResult;
  }
}
```

In this example, search results are stored in a mapping that associates queries with an array of results. The getTopResult function returns the highest-ranked result based on the score assigned to each entry.

Designing Token-Based Incentives

To motivate nodes to contribute to crawling and indexing, a token-based incentive system can be implemented. Tokens serve as a form of reward that is distributed to nodes based on their contribution to the network. For example, nodes that crawl and index web pages, store data in IPFS, or process search queries can earn tokens as compensation.

The following table outlines the incentive structure

Contribution Type	Reward Type	Calculation
Crawling	Tokens per crawled page	Fixed rate per successful crawl
Indexing	Tokens per indexed entry	Based on data size and importance
Storage	Tokens for storing data	Based on data size and retention period
Query Processing	Tokens for processing search queries	Based on processing time and result accuracy

The following Solidity code snippet defines a simple token contract using the ERC20 standard

```
pragma solidity ^0.8.0;
import "@openzeppelin/contracts/token/ERC20/ERC20.sol";

contract SearchToken is ERC20 {
   constructor() ERC20("SearchToken", "STK") {
     _mint(msg.sender, 1000000 * 10 ** decimals());
   }
}
```

By using token-based incentives, the network can attract more participants, increase data coverage, and improve the accuracy and relevance of search results.

Chapter 5

Introduction to AI in Search

Artificial intelligence (AI) has transformed the search industry by improving the accuracy, relevance, and user experience of search engines. Traditional search engines primarily rely on keyword matching and manual ranking algorithms, which often result in irrelevant or incomplete search results. AI introduces a more intelligent and adaptive approach by understanding user intent, learning from search patterns, and dynamically improving the ranking of search results based on user behavior. In a decentralized search environment, AI can play a crucial role in optimizing search performance without relying on a central authority.

This chapter explores the integration of AI in search engines, focusing on four key areas natural language processing (NLP) for query understanding, machine learning (ML) models for ranking and personalization, reinforcement learning for improving search relevance, and neural networks for contextual search understanding. Sample implementations using TensorFlow and PyTorch are provided to demonstrate how AI models can be integrated into a decentralized search infrastructure.

Natural Language Processing (NLP)

Natural Language Processing (NLP) allows search engines to understand the meaning and context behind user queries rather than relying solely on keyword matching. Traditional search engines treat search queries as strings of characters, focusing on direct keyword matches. In contrast, NLP-based search engines process queries as human language, analyzing syntax, semantics, and context to derive the user's actual intent.

For example, a user searching for "best electric cars under $30,000" may expect the search engine to understand the following elements

- The term "best" implies a ranking or comparison based on quality or performance.
- "Electric cars" refers to a specific category of vehicles, requiring classification of indexed content.
- "Under $30,000" introduces a price constraint that the search engine must apply when ranking results.

The process of NLP-based query understanding can be broken down into the following steps

Tokenization – The query is broken down into individual words or tokens.

Lemmatization – Words are reduced to their root forms (e.g., "cars" becomes "car").

Part-of-Speech Tagging – Each token is tagged with its grammatical role (e.g., noun, verb).

Named Entity Recognition – Entities such as product names, prices, and locations are identified.

Dependency Parsing – The grammatical structure of the query is analyzed to identify relationships between words.

The following Python code demonstrates a simple NLP pipeline using the spaCy library to analyze a sample query

```python
import spacy

# Load the language model
nlp = spacy.load("en_core_web_sm")

# Sample query
query = "Best electric cars under $30,000"

# Process the query
doc = nlp(query)

# Tokenization, Lemmatization, and POS tagging
for token in doc
    print(f"Token    {token.text}, Lemma    {token.lemma_}, POS {token.pos_}")

# Named Entity Recognition
for ent in doc.ents
    print(f"Entity {ent.text}, Label {ent.label_}")
```

The output of this code would identify "electric cars" as a product category and "$30,000" as a price constraint. The search engine can then use this structured understanding to refine the search results.

The following table summarizes how NLP processes different types of user queries

Query Example	NLP Processing Steps	Expected Output
"best laptops under $1000"	Tokenization, Lemmatization, Named Entity Recognition	Category = Laptops, Price = $1000
"restaurants near Central Park"	Tokenization, Named Entity Recognition, Dependency Parsing	Category = Restaurants, Location = Central Park
"how to bake a cake"	Tokenization, Lemmatization, Part-of-Speech Tagging	Action = Bake, Object = Cake

By using NLP to process user queries, search engines can deliver more relevant and accurate search results even when the user's query is ambiguous or conversational.

Machine Learning (ML) Models for Ranking

Machine learning (ML) enables search engines to improve the ranking and personalization of search results by learning from user behavior and feedback. Traditional ranking algorithms rely on static rules, such as keyword density and link popularity, which do not adapt to changing user preferences or search patterns. ML-based ranking models, in contrast, continuously adjust and optimize the ranking criteria based on observed data.

ML models used in search ranking typically rely on supervised learning, where the model is trained using labeled data consisting of search queries and the corresponding user-clicked results. The model learns the correlation between query features and the relevance of different search results.

A common approach to ML-based ranking is to use a pairwise or listwise ranking model, where the model compares two or more search results and predicts which one is more relevant.

The following TensorFlow code snippet demonstrates a simple supervised learning model for ranking search results

```
import tensorflow as tf
from tensorflow.keras import layers
```

```
# Sample data (features and labels)
features = [[0.2, 0.8], [0.5, 0.5], [0.9, 0.1]]
labels = [1, 0, 1]

# Define model architecture
model = tf.keras.Sequential([
    layers.Dense(64, activation='relu'),
    layers.Dense(32, activation='relu'),
    layers.Dense(1, activation='sigmoid')
])

# Compile and train the model
model.compile(optimizer='adam',        loss='binary_crossentropy',
metrics=['accuracy'])
model.fit(features, labels, epochs=10)

# Predict relevance score for a new search result
new_feature = [[0.7, 0.3]]
score = model.predict(new_feature)
print("Relevance Score ", score)
```

This model takes a set of features (such as keyword relevance, click-through rate, and page authority) and predicts a relevance score for each search result. The search engine can then use these scores to rank the results dynamically.

The following table outlines typical features used in ML-based ranking models

Feature Type	Description	Example
Content-based	Analyzes the content of the web page	Keyword density, metadata
Link-based	Evaluates the authority of the page	Backlink count, PageRank
User behavior	Analyzes how users interact with the page	Click-through rate, dwell time

Learning for Improving Search Relevance

Reinforcement learning (RL) enables search engines to improve search relevance by learning from user feedback. In RL, the search engine acts as an agent that explores different ranking strategies and receives feedback based on user behavior. Positive feedback (e.g., clicks, long dwell time) reinforces the current ranking strategy, while negative feedback (e.g., bounce rate) encourages the model to explore alternative strategies.

Neural Networks for Contextual Search

Neural networks enhance search engines' ability to understand complex search queries and deliver highly contextualized results. Unlike traditional keyword-based models, neural networks analyze the semantic relationships between words, allowing the search engine to handle natural language queries more effectively.

For example, the following PyTorch code snippet demonstrates a simple neural network for contextual search understanding

```python
import torch
import torch.nn as nn

# Define the model
class SearchNN(nn.Module)
    def __init__(self)
        super(SearchNN, self).__init__()
        self.fc = nn.Sequential(
            nn.Linear(10, 64),
            nn.ReLU(),
            nn.Linear(64, 32),
            nn.ReLU(),
            nn.Linear(32, 1)
        )
    def forward(self, x)
        return self.fc(x)

# Create model and sample input
model = SearchNN()
input_data = torch.randn(1, 10)
output = model(input_data)
print("Relevance Score ", output.item())
```

The neural network assigns relevance scores to search results based on learned patterns, improving the contextual relevance of the returned results. By integrating NLP, machine learning, reinforcement learning, and neural networks into a decentralized search engine, it is possible to build a highly adaptive and accurate search infrastructure that continuously improves based on user behavior and query patterns.

Chapter 6

Combining Blockchain and AI for Search Ranking

Search engines have traditionally faced the challenge of balancing relevance and transparency in search result rankings. Traditional search algorithms are primarily centralized, meaning that the data, ranking criteria, and user behavior metrics are controlled by a single authority. This creates issues of bias, censorship, and manipulation, as the ranking process is not always transparent to end users. By combining artificial intelligence (AI) with blockchain technology, it is possible to create a search ranking system that is both intelligent and transparent. AI improves the relevance and accuracy of search results by analyzing user behavior and understanding complex queries, while blockchain ensures that the ranking process remains auditable, tamper-proof, and decentralized.

This chapter explores how to create a search ranking algorithm that combines blockchain transparency with AI-driven relevance. The key components of this approach include using AI models to score search results based on relevance and authority, storing AI training data and models on a decentralized network, adjusting search rankings through smart contract-based user feedback, and rewarding contributors using blockchain-based tokens. Example implementations using Scikit-learn for AI modeling and Solidity for blockchain-based smart contracts are provided to give readers a practical understanding of how to develop such a system.

AI Models for Scoring Search Results

AI models enhance search ranking by predicting the relevance and authority of search results based on a wide range of features, including user behavior, content quality, and contextual relevance. In a traditional search engine, the ranking algorithm evaluates factors such as keyword density, metadata, and backlink count to assign a relevance score to each search result. AI models improve upon this approach by learning complex patterns from historical data and user feedback.

The scoring process can be structured into three main components

Relevance Score – The AI model evaluates the relevance of a search result based on the semantic similarity between the query and the content of the web page. Natural language processing (NLP) models are commonly used to compute this score by analyzing the textual content, headings, and metadata of the search result.

Authority Score – The AI model assigns an authority score based on external factors such as backlink quality, domain authority, and user engagement metrics. Link-based ranking models like Google's PageRank use a similar approach, but AI models can incorporate more complex patterns and adjust dynamically based on real-time data.

Personalization Score – AI models tailor search results to individual users based on their previous search history, location, and behavior patterns. Reinforcement learning techniques can be used to optimize this personalization score over time.

A sample implementation using Scikit-learn to create a ranking model based on these three components is shown below

```
import numpy as np
from sklearn.ensemble import RandomForestRegressor

# Sample training data  [Relevance, Authority, Personalization]
X_train = np.array([
    [0.8, 0.9, 0.7],
    [0.5, 0.6, 0.4],
    [0.9, 0.8, 0.6]
])

# Labels (actual ranking scores)
y_train = np.array([0.9, 0.5, 0.8])

# Create and train the model
model = RandomForestRegressor(n_estimators=100)
model.fit(X_train, y_train)

# Predict ranking score for a new search result
new_data = np.array([[0.7, 0.8, 0.5]])
score = model.predict(new_data)
```

```
print("Predicted Ranking Score ", score)
```

In this example, the RandomForestRegressor model takes three input features (relevance, authority, and personalization) and predicts an overall ranking score. The model learns from historical user behavior and content quality to generate accurate ranking predictions.

The table below summarizes how different AI models contribute to search ranking

AI Model	Purpose	Example Use Case
Random Forest	Predicting ranking scores based on multiple features	Predicting the rank of search results based on relevance, authority, and user behavior
Neural Network	Learning complex patterns in user behavior	Adapting search results based on evolving user preferences
Support Vector Machine (SVM)	Classifying search results into relevant and non-relevant categories	Binary classification of search relevance
Reinforcement	Improving search	Adjusting search

AI Model	Purpose	Example Use Case
Learning	ranking through feedback-based learning	ranking based on user clicks and bounce rates

Storing AI Training Data and Models

One of the primary challenges in centralized search engines is the control over user data and ranking algorithms by a single entity. AI models require large datasets for training, which are typically stored on centralized servers controlled by a few large organizations. This introduces privacy risks and potential bias in the search results. A decentralized search engine solves this problem by storing AI training data and models on a blockchain-based network, ensuring transparency, security, and user control over data.

Blockchain enables data storage and access using a distributed ledger, where each data entry is time-stamped and cryptographically signed to prevent tampering. AI models can be stored on an InterPlanetary File System (IPFS) or similar decentralized storage network. The model weights and training data can be encoded into blockchain transactions, ensuring that updates to the model are publicly verifiable.

The following diagram illustrates how AI models and training data are stored on a decentralized network

 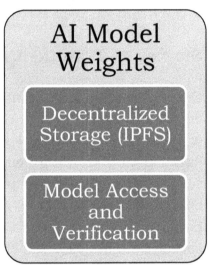

Adjusting Search Ranking Through Feedback

Smart contracts provide a mechanism for incorporating user feedback into the search ranking process in a decentralized manner. A smart contract is a self-executing agreement stored on a blockchain that automatically executes based on predefined conditions. In a decentralized search engine, smart contracts can be used to adjust search rankings based on user engagement, such as clicks, dwell time, and bounce rates.

For example, if a search result consistently receives high engagement (e.g., long dwell time), the smart contract can increase the ranking score of that result. Conversely, if users frequently abandon a search result, the smart contract can reduce its ranking score.

A sample Solidity smart contract that adjusts ranking scores based on user feedback is shown below

```solidity
pragma solidity ^0.8.0;

contract SearchRanking {
    mapping (uint256 => uint256) public rankingScores;

    function updateRanking(uint256 resultId, bool positiveFeedback) public {
        if (positiveFeedback) {
            rankingScores[resultId] += 1;
        } else {
            if (rankingScores[resultId] > 0) {
                rankingScores[resultId] -= 1;
            }
        }
    }
}
```

In this example, the updateRanking function increases the score of a search result if positive feedback is received and decreases the score if negative feedback is recorded.

Using Blockchain-Based Reward Systems

To encourage user participation and contribution to the search ecosystem, blockchain-based tokens can be used to reward contributors. Users who provide useful feedback, validate search results, or improve the AI models can receive tokens as compensation. This creates a self-sustaining ecosystem where users have a direct stake in improving the quality of search results.

Tokens can be distributed through smart contracts based on predefined rules. For example, users who report low-quality search results or contribute high-quality content can receive token rewards. The token economy also creates a feedback loop where high-quality contributions are incentivized, leading to continuous improvement in search quality.

The table below outlines possible incentive mechanisms

Contribution Type	Incentive Mechanism	Example
Providing Feedback	Token Reward	Reporting spammy content
Improving AI Model	Token Reward	Contributing model updates

Contribution Type	Incentive Mechanism	Example
Validating Search Results	Staking Mechanism	Confirming search result quality

By combining AI-driven search relevance with blockchain-based transparency and incentives, a decentralized search engine can deliver both high-quality results and user trust. AI ensures that search results are contextually accurate and personalized, while blockchain ensures that the ranking process remains fair, transparent, and resistant to manipulation.

Chapter 7

Decentralized Indexing and Data Storage

The core of any search engine is its ability to index and store data efficiently. Traditional search engines rely on centralized databases and data centers to store and retrieve information. This centralized architecture, while effective in delivering fast search results, creates several limitations. It introduces a single point of failure, exposes user data to potential privacy breaches, and concentrates control over search ranking and indexing in the hands of a few large corporations. A decentralized search engine, by contrast, distributes the indexing and storage processes across a peer-to-peer (P2P) network. This creates a system that is more secure, resilient, and resistant to censorship.

Decentralized indexing and storage work by distributing data and indexing information across a blockchain-based or peer-to-peer network. This ensures that no single entity controls the search infrastructure, enhancing transparency and reducing the risk of manipulation or data loss. This chapter explores how to build a decentralized data indexing and storage model using peer-to-peer protocols for crawling and indexing, efficient data storage solutions like IPFS (InterPlanetary File System) and Swarm, cryptographic hashing for data integrity, and Merkle trees for fast data retrieval. Practical implementations using Python for crawling and indexing, IPFS for storage, and Solidity for smart contract-based indexing will be provided to give readers a hands-on understanding of how to develop such a system.

Crawling and Indexing Using Peer-to-Peer Protocols

In a traditional search engine, crawling and indexing are performed by a centralized system of web crawlers, which are programs that navigate the web and collect data for indexing. This centralized approach limits scalability and introduces a single point of control. In a decentralized search engine, crawling and indexing are distributed across a peer-to-peer (P2P) network.

A peer-to-peer network allows each node to function both as a client and a server, creating a self-sustaining system where data is continuously collected, indexed, and distributed without reliance on a central authority. This approach improves scalability and fault tolerance since the network can dynamically adapt to changes in data volume and node availability.

A decentralized crawler operates by assigning crawling tasks to nodes in the network. Each node is responsible for crawling a specific set of web pages, extracting metadata, and sharing the results with other nodes. The crawled data is then indexed using a distributed hash table (DHT), which allows for fast lookup of indexed data across the network.

The following Python code demonstrates a simple implementation of a decentralized crawler using the socket library for peer-to-peer communication

```python
import socket
import threading

def handle_peer_connection(conn, addr)
    print(f"Connected to {addr}")
    data = conn.recv(1024).decode()
    print(f"Received data  {data}")
    # Simulate crawling and indexing
    indexed_data = f"Indexed  {data}"
    conn.send(indexed_data.encode())
    conn.close()

def start_server()
    server = socket.socket(socket.AF_INET, socket.SOCK_STREAM)
    server.bind(('localhost', 5000))
    server.listen(5)
    print("Peer node is listening for connections...")

    while True
        conn, addr = server.accept()
        threading.Thread(target=handle_peer_connection,
args=(conn, addr)).start()

# Start the peer node
start_server()
```

This example sets up a peer node that listens for incoming connections and processes crawling tasks. When data is received, the node indexes it and sends the indexed data back to the requesting node. Multiple nodes can be connected to create a peer-to-peer crawling network where each node contributes to the indexing process.

The table below illustrates the structure of a peer-to-peer crawling system

Component	Description
Peer Node	Individual node responsible for crawling and indexing data
Distributed Hash Table (DHT)	Lookup table that stores indexed data across the network
Routing Protocol	Protocol for directing crawling tasks to specific nodes
Data Exchange	Mechanism for sharing indexed data among nodes

Efficient Data Storage Using IPFS and Swarm

Once the data has been crawled and indexed, it must be stored in a decentralized manner to ensure accessibility, resilience, and data security. Traditional search engines store indexed data in centralized data centers, which makes them vulnerable to outages and data loss. Decentralized storage solutions such as the

76

InterPlanetary File System (IPFS) and Swarm provide an alternative approach by distributing data across a network of nodes.

IPFS is a peer-to-peer protocol that stores files and data using a content-addressable system. Instead of relying on URLs or file paths, IPFS assigns a unique cryptographic hash to each piece of data. This ensures that data is immutable and tamper-proof since any change to the data would result in a different hash. When a user requests data, the IPFS network retrieves the file from the node(s) storing it based on its hash.

The following Python code demonstrates how to upload and retrieve files using IPFS

```python
import ipfshttpclient

# Connect to the IPFS network
client = ipfshttpclient.connect('/ip4/127.0.0.1/tcp/5001')

# Upload a file to IPFS
file_hash = client.add('example.txt')['Hash']
print(f"File uploaded to IPFS with hash {file_hash}")

# Retrieve file from IPFS
file_content = client.cat(file_hash).decode()
print(f"Retrieved file content {file_content}")
```

In this example, the ipfshttpclient library is used to connect to an IPFS node, upload a file, and retrieve the file using its unique hash. The hash functions as a permanent identifier, ensuring that the data remains accessible even if the original node storing it goes offline.

The table below compares IPFS and Swarm

Feature	IPFS	Swarm
Storage Model	Content-addressed	Content-addressed
Data Availability	Redundant copies across nodes	Incentive-based storage
Access Mechanism	Direct hash lookup	Incentivized retrieval
Privacy	Public unless encrypted	Encryption-supported

Swarm operates similarly to IPFS but incorporates an incentive layer that rewards nodes for storing and serving data. This creates a self-sustaining ecosystem where storage providers are compensated with cryptocurrency tokens for contributing to the network's storage capacity.

Data Integrity Using Cryptographic Hashing

Ensuring the integrity of indexed and stored data is critical in a decentralized search engine. Cryptographic hashing provides a mechanism for verifying that the data has not been altered or corrupted. A cryptographic hash function takes an input (such as a web page) and produces a fixed-length output (hash) that uniquely represents the input data. Any modification to the data will produce a completely different hash value, making tampering easily detectable.

The following Python code demonstrates the generation of a SHA-256 hash for data integrity verification

```
import hashlib

data = "This is sample data"
hash_object = hashlib.sha256(data.encode())
hash_value = hash_object.hexdigest()
print(f'SHA-256 Hash  {hash_value}")
```

The output hash value serves as a unique fingerprint for the data. When storing data in IPFS or Swarm, the hash value can be used to verify that the retrieved data matches the original input.

Fast Retrieval of Indexed Data

A Merkle tree is a binary tree in which each leaf node represents a hash of a data block, and each non-leaf node represents the hash of its child nodes. Merkle trees enable fast verification of data integrity and efficient data retrieval in a decentralized network. When a user requests a piece of data, the Merkle tree allows the network to verify the data's integrity by comparing the requested data's hash with the hashes stored in the tree.

The diagram below illustrates the structure of a Merkle tree

```
      Root Hash
     /     \
  Hash A      Hash B
  /  \      /  \
 H1   H2   H3   H4
```

Each data block (H1, H2, H3, H4) is hashed, and the resulting hashes are combined to create higher-level hashes until a single root hash is formed. By combining distributed crawling and indexing with efficient decentralized storage and cryptographic integrity checks, a decentralized search engine can deliver fast, secure, and transparent search results. This approach eliminates central points of failure and creates a search ecosystem that is controlled and sustained by the community rather than a single entity.

Chapter 8

Tokenomics and Incentive Models

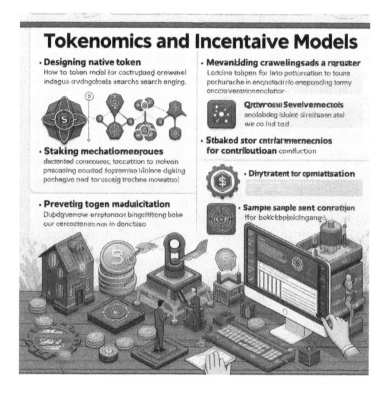

Designing a decentralized search engine requires more than just technical infrastructure and data indexing. For a decentralized network to sustain itself and grow organically, there must be a robust incentive model that motivates participants to contribute computing power, bandwidth, and storage. Tokenomics—the economic system surrounding the creation, distribution, and utility of tokens within a decentralized network—plays a critical role in ensuring that all participants are fairly rewarded for their contributions. A well-designed tokenomics model creates a self-sustaining ecosystem where network participants are incentivized to operate crawling nodes, store indexed data, and process search queries efficiently.

A decentralized search engine relies on a token-based incentive model to reward crawlers and indexers for their work. This ensures that participants remain motivated to contribute to the network even as its size and complexity grow. Tokens serve as the native currency of the ecosystem, allowing participants to earn and spend them based on their level of contribution. This chapter explores the design and implementation of a native token, staking mechanisms for query processing nodes, smart contracts for distributing rewards, and consensus-based methods to prevent token manipulation. Real-world examples using Solidity and ERC-20 token standards will provide a detailed understanding of how to implement a fully functional token-based incentive model.

Native Token for Rewarding Crawlers

In a decentralized search engine, data crawling and indexing are essential for maintaining an up-to-date and efficient search experience. However, without an incentive model, network participants would have little motivation to dedicate their computing resources to these tasks. A native token creates a financial incentive for participants to operate crawling and indexing nodes.

The native token can be designed as an ERC-20 token on the Ethereum blockchain, which provides a standardized framework for fungible tokens. When a node successfully crawls or indexes new data, it is rewarded with a predetermined amount of tokens based on the complexity and value of the data indexed. Similarly, when a user submits a search query and receives accurate results, the indexing node that processed the request earns a token reward.

The reward distribution process can be structured as follows

Action	Reward Calculation	Token Distribution

Action	Reward Calculation	Token Distribution
Crawling	Based on the size and uniqueness of the data crawled	Direct token reward from the network
Indexing	Based on the relevance and accuracy of the indexed data	Direct token reward from the network
Query Processing	Based on the speed and accuracy of query resolution	Token reward split between processing nodes

To create an ERC-20 token for the network, the following Solidity code can be used

```solidity
// SPDX-License-Identifier MIT
pragma solidity ^0.8.0;

import "@openzeppelin/contracts/token/ERC20/ERC20.sol";
import "@openzeppelin/contracts/access/Ownable.sol";

contract SearchToken is ERC20, Ownable {
    constructor(uint256 initialSupply) ERC20("SearchToken", "SRT") {
        _mint(msg.sender, initialSupply);
    }

    function rewardCrawlers(address crawler, uint256 amount) public onlyOwner {
        _mint(crawler, amount);
```

```
    }

    function rewardIndexers(address indexer, uint256 amount)
public onlyOwner {
        _mint(indexer, amount);
    }
}
```

In this example, the SearchToken contract creates a
fungible token based on the ERC-20 standard. The
contract allows the network owner (or a decentralized
autonomous organization, DAO) to mint new tokens
and distribute them as rewards to crawlers and
indexers. The rewardCrawlers and rewardIndexers
functions enable direct reward payments, while the
token supply is managed dynamically based on
network performance and contribution levels.

To avoid token inflation, the total supply of tokens
should be capped, and rewards should be adjusted
based on the overall size and performance of the
network. The tokenomics model should incorporate a
gradual reduction in reward rates as the network
matures, ensuring long-term sustainability.

Staking Mechanisms for Query Processing

Staking mechanisms are used to secure the network
and ensure that query processing nodes remain
reliable and trustworthy. In a staking model, nodes are
required to lock up a certain amount of tokens as

collateral before they are allowed to process queries. This discourages malicious behavior and ensures that nodes have a financial stake in the accuracy and efficiency of their responses.

When a node processes a query, the correctness and speed of the response are evaluated by the network. If the node provides an accurate response within the expected timeframe, it earns additional tokens as a reward. If the node fails to provide a valid response or engages in malicious behavior (e.g., providing false data), a portion of its staked tokens may be confiscated as a penalty.

The following Solidity code demonstrates a staking contract for query processing nodes

```solidity
// SPDX-License-Identifier  MIT
pragma solidity ^0.8.0;

contract StakingContract {
    mapping(address => uint256) public stakes;
    address public token;

    constructor(address _token) {
        token = _token;
    }

    function stakeTokens(uint256 amount) public {
        IERC20(token).transferFrom(msg.sender,        address(this), amount);
        stakes[msg.sender] += amount;
```

```
    }

    function withdrawTokens(uint256 amount) public {
        require(stakes[msg.sender] >= amount, "Insufficient stake");
        stakes[msg.sender] -= amount;
        IERC20(token).transfer(msg.sender, amount);
    }

    function rewardNode(address node, uint256 reward) public {
        require(stakes[node] > 0, "Node is not staked");
        IERC20(token).transfer(node, reward);
    }

    function slashStake(address node, uint256 penalty) public {
        require(stakes[node] >= penalty, "Insufficient stake");
        stakes[node] -= penalty;
        IERC20(token).transfer(msg.sender, penalty);
    }
}
```

This contract allows nodes to stake tokens, withdraw tokens, and receive rewards for query processing. The slashStake function penalizes nodes for providing false data or failing to respond in a timely manner, creating a financial deterrent against malicious behavior.

The table below illustrates the staking process

Action	Stake Requirement	Outcome
Successful	Minimum stake	Earn additional

Action	Stake Requirement	Outcome
Query	met	tokens
Failed Query	Minimum stake met	Penalty applied to stake
Malicious Behavior	Minimum stake met	Complete stake forfeiture

Smart Contracts to Distribute Rewards

To automate the reward distribution process, smart contracts can be created to evaluate node performance and distribute tokens accordingly. When a query is processed, the smart contract measures the accuracy and speed of the response and allocates rewards to the contributing nodes.

The following Solidity contract distributes rewards based on contribution

```
// SPDX-License-Identifier MIT
pragma solidity ^0.8.0;

contract RewardContract {
    address public token;

    constructor(address _token) {
```

```
    token = _token;
    }

    function distributeReward(address recipient, uint256 amount)
public {
        IERC20(token).transfer(recipient, amount);
    }
}
```

The reward contract interacts with the staking contract to calculate rewards based on the contribution level and performance of the node. If the node processes a complex query with high accuracy and low latency, it receives a higher token reward.

Preventing Token Manipulation

Token manipulation is a major threat to decentralized ecosystems. Without a robust consensus mechanism, malicious nodes could inflate token rewards, double-spend tokens, or falsify indexing and query processing data. Blockchain consensus mechanisms such as Proof of Stake (PoS) and Proof of Work (PoW) prevent manipulation by requiring network participants to solve cryptographic puzzles or lock up tokens to validate transactions.

A PoS-based model is ideal for decentralized search engines because it encourages long-term participation while reducing energy consumption. In a PoS-based model, nodes that hold more tokens have greater influence over the validation process, creating a financial incentive for honest behavior. Malicious nodes are deterred by the risk of losing their staked tokens if they attempt to manipulate the system.

The following table compares PoS and PoW for decentralized search engines

Mechanism	Security	Energy Consumption	Incentive Model
Proof of Stake (PoS)	High	Low	Staking-based rewards
Proof of Work (PoW)	High	High	Mining-based rewards

By combining a well-designed token model, staking mechanisms, automated reward distribution, and blockchain-based consensus, a decentralized search engine can create a self-sustaining economic model. This ensures that participants are motivated to contribute resources, provide accurate data, and improve network performance over time.

Chapter 9

Privacy and Security in Decentralized Search

Ensuring privacy and security in a decentralized search engine is one of the most critical aspects of building a trustworthy and sustainable platform. In traditional search engines, user data is often harvested, stored, and monetized without the user's consent. Personal search histories, browsing patterns, and IP addresses are frequently collected, creating serious privacy risks. Additionally, centralized search engines present a single point of failure, making them vulnerable to hacking, surveillance, and data leaks. A decentralized search engine solves these problems by distributing the data and search processing tasks across a network of independent nodes, eliminating central control and improving security. However, decentralization introduces new challenges in securing data transmission, verifying search integrity, and protecting user privacy.

This chapter explores how to implement end-to-end encryption for search queries and results, use zero-knowledge proofs for secure data verification, prevent Sybil attacks and double-spending through Proof of Stake (PoS) consensus, and handle data privacy requests using smart contracts. Detailed sample implementations using zk-SNARKs (Zero-Knowledge Succinct Non-Interactive Arguments of Knowledge) and IPFS (InterPlanetary File System) will be included to provide a practical understanding of these advanced security techniques.

Implementing End-to-End Encryption

End-to-end encryption (E2EE) ensures that search queries and results remain private and accessible only to the user who initiated the search. In a traditional search engine, user queries are sent to a central server, processed, and stored in plaintext. This makes the data vulnerable to interception, unauthorized access, and data leaks. In a decentralized search engine, E2EE eliminates these vulnerabilities by encrypting search data at the source and decrypting it only at the client side.

The encryption process can be implemented using asymmetric cryptography, where the user generates a pair of public and private keys. The search query is encrypted using the public key, and only the user's private key can decrypt the search results. This prevents intermediary nodes, including crawlers and indexers, from accessing the search content.

The encryption process can be illustrated as follows

User Request The user generates a search query and encrypts it using their public key.

Transmission The encrypted query is transmitted through the network of indexing and crawling nodes.

Processing Indexing nodes search the data and generate encrypted results.

Decryption The user decrypts the search results using their private key.

The encryption and decryption process can be implemented using RSA (Rivest-Shamir-Adleman) encryption in Solidity

```
// SPDX-License-Identifier  MIT
pragma solidity ^0.8.0;

import
"@openzeppelin/contracts/utils/cryptography/ECDSA.sol";

contract SearchEncryption {
    using ECDSA for bytes32;

    function encryptQuery(bytes32    query,    bytes    memory
publicKey) public pure returns (bytes32) {
        return query.toEthSignedMessageHash().recover(publicKey);
    }

    function decryptResult(bytes32 encryptedResult, bytes memory
privateKey) public pure returns (bytes32) {
        return
encryptedResult.toEthSignedMessageHash().recover(privateKey);
    }
}
```

In this example, the encryptQuery function encrypts the search query using the user's public key, while the decryptResult function decrypts the search result using the private key. The encryption ensures that even if an intermediary node intercepts the data, it cannot be decrypted without the user's private key.

The encryption model can be summarized as follows

Stage	Action	Security Level
Encryption	Query encrypted with public key	High
Transmission	Encrypted query sent through network	High
Processing	Encrypted result generated	High
Decryption	Result decrypted with private key	High

This encryption model ensures that the search data remains private and secure throughout the entire process, even if an intermediary node is compromised.

Using Zero-Knowledge Proofs for Secure Data

Zero-Knowledge Proofs (ZKPs) provide a method for verifying the authenticity and correctness of search data without revealing the underlying information. In a decentralized search engine, ZKPs allow a node to prove that a search result is accurate without exposing the actual search content or the source of the data. This protects user privacy while maintaining the integrity of the search results.

zk-SNARKs (Zero-Knowledge Succinct Non-Interactive Arguments of Knowledge) are a specific type of ZKP that allows one party to prove to another that they possess certain knowledge without revealing the content of that knowledge. For example, in a decentralized search engine, a zk-SNARK can be used to verify that a search query was processed correctly without revealing the query itself.

The zk-SNARK process works as follows

Prover Generation The node generating the search result creates a zk-SNARK proof that verifies the accuracy of the search result.

Proof Transmission The zk-SNARK proof is transmitted to the user along with the encrypted search result.

Verification The user's client verifies the zk-SNARK proof to confirm the validity of the search result without revealing the query or the result content.

A zk-SNARK contract can be implemented using Solidity as follows

```solidity
// SPDX-License-Identifier  MIT
pragma solidity ^0.8.0;

import "@openzeppelin/contracts/cryptography/ECDSA.sol";

contract zkSNARK {
    using ECDSA for bytes32;

    function generateProof(bytes32 queryHash) public pure returns
(bytes32) {
        return queryHash.toEthSignedMessageHash();
    }

    function verifyProof(bytes32 proof, bytes32 queryHash) public
pure returns (bool) {
        return proof.toEthSignedMessageHash() == queryHash;
    }
}
```

This contract creates a zk-SNARK proof by hashing the query and generating a cryptographic signature. The verifyProof function checks if the proof matches the original query hash, confirming the validity of the search result without exposing the query content.

Preventing Sybil Attacks

A Sybil attack occurs when a malicious entity creates multiple fake nodes to manipulate the network by generating false search results or hijacking query processing. A double-spending attack involves spending the same token or resource more than once, which undermines the integrity of the token-based incentive model.

Proof of Stake (PoS) consensus prevents these attacks by requiring nodes to stake tokens as collateral. In a PoS-based decentralized search engine, nodes must lock up a certain amount of tokens to participate in query processing and indexing. If a node attempts to manipulate search results or engage in double-spending, the staked tokens are forfeited as a penalty.

The staking and slashing process is illustrated below

Action	Stake Requirement	Outcome
Honest Processing	Minimum stake met	Earn tokens
False Data Submission	Minimum stake met	Stake slashed
Double-Spending Attempt	Minimum stake met	Complete stake loss

Handling Data Privacy Requests

Data privacy regulations such as the General Data Protection Regulation (GDPR) require search platforms to provide users with the ability to delete their personal data upon request. In a decentralized search engine, user data can be stored on IPFS (InterPlanetary File System) and managed using smart contracts.

An IPFS-based privacy contract can be structured as follows

```solidity
// SPDX-License-Identifier  MIT
pragma solidity ^0.8.0;

contract PrivacyContract {
    mapping(address => string) public userData;

    function storeData(address user, string memory data) public {
        userData[user] = data;
    }

    function deleteData(address user) public {
        require(msg.sender == user, "Unauthorized");
        delete userData[user];
    }
}
```

In this contract, the storeData function allows users to store encrypted search data. The deleteData function enables the user to delete their data at any time, ensuring compliance with privacy regulations. By combining end-to-end encryption, zero-knowledge proofs, Proof of Stake consensus, and IPFS-based privacy management, a decentralized search engine can provide a high level of privacy and security. This ensures that user data remains protected while maintaining the integrity and efficiency of the search engine's operations.

Chapter 10

Personalization and Context-Aware Search

Personalization in search engines is an essential feature for enhancing user experience by delivering more relevant results tailored to individual preferences, behaviors, and intentions. Traditional search engines often rely on centralized storage of user data, which raises significant privacy concerns. Users are becoming increasingly aware of how their search histories and preferences are tracked and exploited for commercial purposes. In a decentralized search system, it is possible to provide personalized search experiences without compromising user privacy. This chapter will explore how to build personalized search experiences in a decentralized environment, ensuring that privacy is respected while still delivering highly relevant, context-aware results.

This chapter will cover several key techniques for achieving privacy-preserving personalization, including local storage and processing of user search history, federated learning to train AI models without exposing sensitive data, intent detection and context-based ranking to improve result relevance, and user feedback mechanisms that allow the personalization process to adapt based on individual interaction. Practical implementations using TensorFlow and Keras for federated learning will also be provided, offering hands-on insight into how to deploy privacy-preserving AI in decentralized systems.

Local Storage and Processing of User Search

In a decentralized search engine, maintaining user privacy requires innovative approaches to handling search history. Traditional systems store user data on central servers, allowing for the continuous monitoring and accumulation of search histories. In contrast, decentralized search engines must prioritize privacy by storing and processing search histories locally on the user's device. This ensures that sensitive information remains private and is not transferred to a central server or exposed to third-party entities. By processing the data on the user's device, the system can still personalize search results based on previous interactions without violating privacy.

Local storage involves saving the user's search history, preferences, and other relevant information on their local device, either in a secure database or a file system. The key advantage of this approach is that the data never leaves the device, significantly reducing the risk of unauthorized access. However, this requires intelligent processing techniques that allow the system to use the stored data to improve the search experience, even when the data is not centralized.

To enable personalized search on a decentralized system, the search engine must analyze the user's search history locally to identify trends, preferences, and frequent queries. With this information, the system can provide more relevant results, such as highlighting previously searched content or suggesting related topics. This method also allows for real-time personalization, meaning that users will see immediate updates based on their most recent searches without the need for cloud processing.

The flow of data processing in local search history storage is illustrated as follows

Stage	Action	Security Level
Data Storage	User search history saved locally	High
Local Processing	Search results personalized based on stored history	High
Personalization	Adjust results in real-time without cloud storage	High

Federated Learning to Train AI Models

Federated learning is a cutting-edge machine learning technique that enables the training of AI models across multiple devices without the need for data to be shared between them. Instead of sending raw user data to a central server, federated learning allows each

104

device to independently train a model on its local dataset and then share only the model's updates (i.e., gradients) to the central server for aggregation. This technique ensures that sensitive user data remains on the device, which aligns with privacy requirements while still enabling the model to learn from diverse data sources.

In the context of a decentralized search engine, federated learning can be used to build personalization models that learn from a user's search history, preferences, and behaviors. The model can then provide personalized search rankings without compromising privacy because the search data is never exposed or centralized. The central server or aggregation mechanism only learns from model updates, and the actual data—such as search queries or click-through rates—remains private.

Federated learning works in the following way

Model Initialization The central server sends a base model to each user device.

Local Training Each device trains the model using local data, such as search history, query clicks, and interaction feedback, but without sharing any raw data.

Model Aggregation Each device sends only the model updates (e.g., gradients) back to the central server, where they are aggregated to form a global model.

Model Deployment The global model is then redistributed to all participating devices for further local training.

In the context of personalized search, this allows the search engine to constantly improve its recommendations and search ranking algorithms based on user behavior, while maintaining strict data privacy.

Here's an example implementation of federated learning using TensorFlow and Keras

```
import tensorflow as tf
from tensorflow import keras
from tensorflow_federated import learning

# Define a simple model for federated learning
def model_fn()
    model = keras.Sequential([
        keras.layers.Dense(64, activation='relu', input_shape=(10,)),
        keras.layers.Dense(10, activation='softmax')
    ])
    model.compile(optimizer='adam',
loss='sparse_categorical_crossentropy', metrics=['accuracy'])
    return model

# Federated averaging function for model aggregation
def server_model_fn()
    model = model_fn()
```

```
    return model

# Use federated learning for model training
federated_data = [local_data_1, local_data_2]   # Example local
datasets
fed_avg = learning.build_federated_averaging_process(model_fn)
state = fed_avg.initialize()

# Train the federated model
for round_num in range(10)
    state, metrics = fed_avg.next(state, federated_data)
    print(f'Round {round_num}, Metrics {metrics}')
```

In this example, the model_fn function defines a basic model for search personalization, and federated learning is applied by using the tensorflow_federated library to perform federated averaging across local datasets. The model is trained without sharing any raw data, ensuring that user privacy is maintained.

Intent Detection and Context-Based Search

Intent detection and context-based search ranking are essential features of a personalized search engine, as they allow the system to understand the user's goals and preferences behind each query. Intent detection refers to the process of analyzing a user's query to determine the underlying purpose or objective. For example, if a user searches for "apple," the intent could be related to the fruit, the technology company, or a specific product.

In a decentralized search system, intent detection can be achieved using natural language processing (NLP) models, such as recurrent neural networks (RNNs) or transformers, which analyze the query in the context of previous searches. By considering the user's search history and contextual information, the system can better rank results that match the user's specific intent. Context-based search ranking takes this further by adjusting the ranking of results based on factors such as location, time, and past search behavior.

The implementation of intent detection could be as follows

Intent Type	Example Query	Action Taken
Informational Intent	"What is the capital of France?"	Provide factual answer
Navigational Intent	"Apple store near me"	Suggest local stores
Transactional Intent	"Buy iPhone online"	Suggest e-commerce sites

By leveraging contextual data such as recent searches, geographic location, or even device type, the search engine can rank results more effectively, ensuring the user receives the most relevant content based on their current needs.

Feedback Mechanisms to Adjust Personalization

User feedback is critical for fine-tuning personalization in a decentralized search engine. This feedback can come in various forms, such as clicks, queries, and ratings. Each user interaction with the search engine provides valuable insights that can be used to adjust the personalization model.

For instance, if a user consistently clicks on certain types of content or interacts with specific types of queries, the system can learn from this behavior and adjust search rankings to prioritize those types of content. By allowing users to directly adjust personalization preferences through settings or feedback mechanisms, a decentralized search engine can provide more accurate and customized results over time.

The feedback loop could be designed as follows

User Interaction The user interacts with search results by clicking on links or rating content.

Data Logging Feedback is logged locally on the device, capturing interaction details (e.g., clicked result, time spent, etc.).

Model Update Based on the feedback, the personalization model is updated either locally or through federated learning to improve the relevance of future results.

A user feedback system can be illustrated in the following table

Feedback Type	Action	Impact on Personalization
Clicks on Search Results	Increase relevance of similar results	Immediate update
Rating of Content	Prioritize content with higher ratings	Long-term trend adjustment
Search History Feedback	Adjust content suggestions based on history	Continuous refinement

This feedback loop ensures that the system continuously improves, providing more relevant results based on individual user interactions.

Personalization and context-aware search in a decentralized environment present unique challenges and opportunities. By utilizing local storage for user search history, federated learning for privacy-preserving model training, intent detection for improved ranking, and user feedback mechanisms for continuous refinement, a decentralized search engine can deliver highly relevant, personalized results without compromising privacy. As we have seen in this chapter, these techniques, when combined effectively, can create a truly user-centric search experience while respecting the core values of decentralization and data privacy.

Chapter 11

Visual and Multimodal Search in a Decentralized Environment

The growing demand for sophisticated search capabilities that extend beyond traditional text-based queries has led to the rise of visual and multimodal search systems. Visual search enables users to search for content using images, videos, or even voice, rather than relying solely on keywords. In a decentralized search engine, where data is distributed and user privacy is paramount, integrating these multimodal search capabilities presents unique challenges and opportunities. This chapter will delve into how to build a decentralized search engine that supports image, video, and voice search while maintaining privacy and ensuring efficiency. It will explore the technical components required to achieve this functionality, including convolutional neural networks (CNNs) for image search, frame-based analysis and AI models for video search, automatic speech recognition (ASR) for voice search, and the integration of multiple input modalities into a cohesive, multimodal search experience.

In a decentralized search engine, each type of input—text, image, voice, and video—can be processed locally on the user's device, thereby maintaining privacy while enabling advanced search capabilities. This chapter will demonstrate how these technologies can be implemented using open-source libraries like TensorFlow and OpenCV, and provide a detailed exploration of how to build the underlying models that power these features.

Search Using Convolutional Neural Networks

Image search is a rapidly growing field that allows users to search for visual content by uploading an image rather than typing in a text query. This functionality is particularly useful in applications like fashion, e-commerce, and digital asset management, where users want to find similar items or content based on visual characteristics. Convolutional Neural Networks (CNNs) have proven to be highly effective for image classification, object detection, and image retrieval tasks.

In a decentralized search engine, image search can be achieved by processing the image query locally on the user's device using a pre-trained CNN model. Once the query image is processed, the CNN model extracts features from the image, such as textures, shapes, and patterns, and compares them with a decentralized index of images stored across the network. Instead of sending the entire image data to a centralized server for comparison, the model can only send feature vectors—compact numerical representations of the image—to a distributed network for efficient retrieval.

The process of image search using CNNs involves several steps

Image Preprocessing The query image is resized, normalized, and converted into a format suitable for input into the CNN model.

Feature Extraction The CNN model processes the image and extracts relevant features, which represent the visual characteristics of the image in a high-dimensional space.

Image Matching The extracted feature vector is compared with the feature vectors of images in the decentralized index to identify the most similar images.

Search Results The system returns a list of images that match the query based on their similarity to the extracted features.

For instance, in TensorFlow, a CNN model for image search might look like this

```
import tensorflow as tf
from tensorflow.keras.preprocessing import image
import numpy as np

# Load the pre-trained CNN model (e.g., ResNet50)
model = tf.keras.applications.ResNet50(weights='imagenet',
include_top=False, pooling='avg')

# Preprocess the image for the CNN
img_path = 'query_image.jpg'
img = image.load_img(img_path, target_size=(224, 224))
img_array = image.img_to_array(img)
img_array = np.expand_dims(img_array, axis=0)
```

```
img_array                                                    =
tf.keras.applications.resnet50.preprocess_input(img_array)

# Extract features using the CNN model
features = model.predict(img_array)
```

In this example, a pre-trained ResNet50 model is used to extract features from the query image. These features can then be compared against the decentralized image index to return similar images.

Video Search Using Frame-Based Analysis

Video search goes beyond static images, requiring analysis of the motion and context within video frames. To enable video search in a decentralized engine, the video is broken down into individual frames, each of which can be analyzed using AI models for object recognition, scene detection, and feature extraction. These frames are then indexed in a decentralized manner, and search queries are processed similarly to image search but at the frame level.

Video search typically involves the following steps

Video Frame Extraction The video is divided into frames, which are images that can be processed independently.

Frame Analysis Each frame is analyzed using convolutional neural networks (CNNs) or other AI models to extract features and identify objects, actions, or scenes.

Frame Indexing The features of each frame are stored in the decentralized index, allowing the search engine to find relevant frames quickly.

Search Results The user's query is compared to the features of the indexed frames, and the most relevant frames or video segments are returned.

Using TensorFlow and OpenCV, the implementation of frame-based video analysis can look like this

```
import cv2
import tensorflow as tf

# Load pre-trained CNN for frame analysis (e.g., MobileNet)
model   =   tf.keras.applications.MobileNetV2(weights='imagenet',
include_top=False, pooling='avg')

# Open the video
video_capture = cv2.VideoCapture('query_video.mp4')

# Extract frames and analyze them
while True
    ret, frame = video_capture.read()
    if not ret
        break

    # Preprocess frame for the CNN
    frame_resized = cv2.resize(frame, (224, 224))
    frame_array = np.expand_dims(frame_resized, axis=0)
```

117

```
frame_array                                    =
tf.keras.applications.mobilenet_v2.preprocess_input(frame_array)

    # Extract features from the frame
    features = model.predict(frame_array)

    # Store features in decentralized index (not shown here)
    # Compare features with indexed video frames (not shown here)

video_capture.release()
```

In this example, we use OpenCV to extract frames from a video file and TensorFlow to process each frame using a pre-trained MobileNetV2 model. The resulting features can then be indexed in a decentralized database, allowing users to search for specific video segments based on their content.

Voice Search Using Automatic Speech Recognition (ASR)

Voice search has become a crucial component of modern search engines, allowing users to query the system using natural language speech. In a decentralized system, implementing voice search involves converting speech into text using automatic speech recognition (ASR) systems, and then processing the resulting text query using traditional search techniques.

The process of voice search in a decentralized search engine involves the following steps

Speech Input The user speaks a query into their device.

Speech Recognition The audio is converted into text using an ASR model, such as Google's Speech-to-Text API or an open-source model like DeepSpeech.

Text-Based Search The text query is then processed and matched with indexed content, just as in traditional text search engines.

Search Results The results are returned based on the relevance of the indexed content.

An example of using an open-source ASR model like DeepSpeech for speech recognition might look like this

```
import deepspeech
import wave
import numpy as np

# Load pre-trained DeepSpeech model
model = deepspeech.Model('deepspeech-0.9.3-models.pbmm')

# Load the audio file
with wave.open('query_audio.wav', 'r') as audio_file
    frames = audio_file.readframes(audio_file.getnframes())
    audio = np.frombuffer(frames, dtype=np.int16)

# Convert audio to text using ASR
text_query = model.stt(audio)
```

```
# Perform text-based search using the query (not shown here)
```

In this example, we use the DeepSpeech ASR model to convert a speech query into text, which can then be processed by the decentralized search engine.

Combining Text, Image and Voice Inputs

A multimodal search engine enables users to combine text, image, and voice queries to retrieve more accurate and relevant results. This involves integrating different types of inputs into a unified search framework, where each modality—text, image, voice, and even video—can contribute to refining the search results.

In a decentralized search system, multimodal search can be achieved by processing each input type independently on the user's device and combining the results based on their relevance. For example, a user might upload an image of a product and say, "I want to buy this," and the system would combine the visual information from the image with the intent expressed in the voice query to deliver a tailored set of search results. This approach requires advanced natural language processing (NLP), image recognition, and ASR models working together.

The integration of multiple modalities might follow this general process

Text Input Process the text query using traditional search techniques.

Image Input Process the image query using a CNN to extract features and search for similar images.

Voice Input Convert the voice query to text using ASR and process it like a text query.

Multimodal Fusion Combine the results from all modalities, considering the relevance of each modality to the user's intent.

This process ensures that users can provide different types of input and receive personalized and contextually appropriate search results.

Incorporating visual, video, and voice search capabilities into a decentralized search engine represents a significant leap forward in user experience. By leveraging advanced AI models such as CNNs for image search, frame-based analysis for video search, and ASR for voice queries, a decentralized system can offer a more versatile and interactive search experience. The use of decentralized storage and processing ensures that user privacy is maintained while providing sophisticated search capabilities. As we move towards a multimodal future, the ability to combine these diverse inputs into a cohesive search experience will be crucial for building the next generation of search engines.

Chapter 12

Smart Contract-Based Governance and Algorithm Transparency

In the rapidly evolving landscape of decentralized technologies, one of the key challenges is ensuring transparency and fairness in the decision-making processes that govern the algorithms driving these systems. For decentralized search engines, the ability to modify and improve algorithms based on community input, while ensuring that changes are transparent and accountable, is essential. Smart contract-based governance presents a solution by enabling stakeholders to participate in decision-making, vote on updates, and ensure that algorithm modifications are auditable and traceable on the blockchain. This chapter will explore how to implement such transparent algorithm governance using smart contracts, allowing token holders to participate in governance decisions, vote on algorithm updates, audit AI model changes, and even create forks based on community feedback.

This chapter will also delve into the technical implementation of these concepts using Solidity, the Ethereum-based smart contract language, and DAO (Decentralized Autonomous Organization) frameworks that facilitate decentralized governance. By combining smart contracts with blockchain transparency, we can create a robust framework for managing and evolving algorithms in a decentralized search engine.

Voting Mechanisms for Algorithm Updates

A key component of smart contract-based governance is the creation of transparent voting mechanisms that allow token holders and community members to participate in the decision-making process regarding algorithm updates. This form of governance ensures that no single entity can unilaterally change the algorithm, fostering a more democratic system. In a decentralized search engine, where algorithmic changes could have a significant impact on the user experience and fairness, it is essential to have a clear and transparent process for voting on updates.

To implement voting on algorithm updates, a smart contract is created that allows token holders to vote on proposed algorithm modifications. The process begins when a proposal is submitted to the contract. This proposal could be a change to the search ranking algorithm, a modification to the AI model used in query processing, or any other update that affects the core functionality of the search engine. Once the proposal is submitted, token holders can vote on it within a set period.

Each token holder's voting power can be proportional to the number of tokens they hold, ensuring that those with a larger stake in the ecosystem have more influence on the outcome of the vote. A threshold percentage of votes (e.g., a simple majority or a supermajority) must be reached for the proposal to pass.

The following Solidity code snippet demonstrates a basic voting mechanism for algorithm updates

```solidity
pragma solidity ^0.8.0;

contract AlgorithmGovernance {
    address public owner;
    mapping(address => uint256) public tokenBalance;
    mapping(address => bool) public voted;
    uint256 public totalVotes;
    uint256 public threshold;
    mapping(uint256 => Proposal) public proposals;
    uint256 public proposalCount;

    struct Proposal {
        string description;
        uint256 voteCount;
        bool isApproved;
    }

    modifier onlyOwner() {
        require(msg.sender == owner, "Only the owner can perform this action.");
        _;
    }

    modifier hasNotVoted() {
        require(!voted[msg.sender], "You have already voted.");
        _;
    }
```

```solidity
constructor() {
    owner = msg.sender;
    threshold = 51; // Simple majority
}

function submitProposal(string memory _description) public
onlyOwner {
    proposalCount++;
    proposals[proposalCount] = Proposal({
        description _description,
        voteCount 0,
        isApproved false
    });
}

function vote(uint256 proposalId) public hasNotVoted {
    require(tokenBalance[msg.sender] > 0, "You need tokens to
vote.");
    proposals[proposalId].voteCount                      +=
tokenBalance[msg.sender];
    voted[msg.sender] = true;
    totalVotes += tokenBalance[msg.sender];
}

function finalizeProposal(uint256 proposalId) public {
    Proposal storage proposal = proposals[proposalId];
    if (proposal.voteCount * 100 / totalVotes >= threshold) {
        proposal.isApproved = true;
    }
}

function setTokenBalance(address user, uint256 balance)
public onlyOwner {
    tokenBalance[user] = balance;
```

```
    }
}
```

In this example, token holders can vote on algorithm proposals, and the proposal is approved if it meets the threshold (e.g., a simple majority). The setTokenBalance function assigns tokens to each user, and the vote function allows them to cast their votes.

Token Holders to Participate in Decisions

In a decentralized system, token holders represent the community of stakeholders. Allowing them to participate in governance decisions ensures that algorithm changes align with the interests of the broader ecosystem. Token-based governance systems have been widely adopted in blockchain ecosystems, where token holders can propose and vote on changes to protocols, updates to smart contracts, or new features.

In the case of a decentralized search engine, token holders can be incentivized to participate in governance by rewarding them with additional tokens or other benefits for their engagement. Token holders could vote on a variety of issues, such as

- Algorithm updates (e.g., changes to ranking or indexing methods)

- Modifications to reward structures (e.g., for crawlers and indexers)
- Proposals for new features or functionalities
- Network upgrades, including infrastructure changes or optimizations

A well-designed governance system must ensure that token holders are motivated to make informed decisions, ensuring that the system remains sustainable and fair over time.

Auditing AI Model Updates Using Blockchain

One of the major advantages of using blockchain for algorithm governance is the ability to audit and trace all changes made to the algorithm. Blockchain provides an immutable ledger of all transactions, including voting outcomes and the actual implementation of changes. This creates a transparent and auditable history of all algorithm updates, ensuring that any modifications can be traced back to the decision-making process that led to them.

Every time an algorithm update is approved and implemented, a transaction is recorded on the blockchain. This record contains information about the specific update (such as a new version of the AI model or changes to the ranking algorithm) and the proposal's voting history, including who voted and how many tokens were involved.

Blockchain transaction logs also enable stakeholders to verify that updates were made according to the community's consensus, preventing malicious actors from introducing unauthorized changes. Furthermore, if an issue arises with a new algorithm version, stakeholders can refer to the transaction logs to determine exactly what changed and who was responsible for approving the update.

To facilitate this, the smart contract governing the voting mechanism could record each decision in the blockchain, creating a permanent record that can be audited later.

Algorithm Forks Based Feedback

In a decentralized environment, it is possible for the community to disagree on a particular algorithmic change. In such cases, a system should allow for the creation of algorithm forks—versions of the algorithm that branch off from the main algorithm, based on different governance decisions. These forks allow different groups within the community to experiment with different approaches and test alternative algorithms, which can later be merged or adopted based on their success.

The process of creating an algorithm fork is similar to that used in blockchain forks. When a significant disagreement arises over an algorithmic update, the community can propose a fork as an alternative version of the algorithm. This fork would be governed by its own set of smart contracts, with its own set of participants who can vote on future updates specific to that fork.

The key advantage of this approach is that it fosters innovation while ensuring that the core system remains decentralized and flexible. In the event that a fork becomes successful or proves to be more effective, it can be adopted into the main algorithm through another governance process, or the community can decide to continue developing it separately.

Smart contract-based governance for decentralized search engines enables transparency, accountability, and inclusivity in algorithmic decision-making. By leveraging blockchain technology, stakeholders can participate in the governance process through voting mechanisms, ensuring that changes to the search engine's algorithms reflect the collective interests of the community. Furthermore, the transparency of blockchain allows for the auditing of AI model updates, providing a clear and immutable record of all algorithmic modifications. The ability to create algorithm forks based on community feedback ensures that the system remains flexible and adaptive, allowing for experimentation and innovation. By integrating these governance mechanisms into a decentralized search engine, we can create a more fair and democratic system that prioritizes the interests of its users while maintaining algorithmic integrity.

Chapter 13

Performance Tuning and Scalability

Building a decentralized search engine introduces unique challenges, particularly in terms of performance tuning and scalability. Traditional search engines rely on centralized servers to handle indexing, query processing, and storage. In a decentralized system, these operations must be distributed across multiple nodes, requiring efficient strategies to ensure the system remains fast and scalable as it grows. This chapter will explore various techniques and strategies to optimize the performance of a decentralized search engine, including sharding, load balancing, caching, and the use of blockchain sidechains. Additionally, we will discuss methods for improving indexing speed and reducing latency while minimizing the overhead associated with consensus mechanisms. By employing these strategies, a decentralized search engine can efficiently handle increasing amounts of data and users without compromising on performance.

Load Balancing Using Blockchain Sidechains

Sharding is one of the most effective techniques for scaling decentralized systems. It involves breaking down a large dataset into smaller, manageable pieces known as "shards." Each shard contains a subset of the data, and these shards can be distributed across multiple nodes in the network. In the context of a decentralized search engine, sharding can be used to divide the index, storage, and crawling tasks among different blockchain sidechains, allowing each sidechain to manage a smaller portion of the data while still contributing to the overall search process.

Sidechains are independent blockchains that are linked to a main blockchain, enabling the offloading of tasks from the main chain to these auxiliary chains. By utilizing sidechains, the load can be distributed efficiently, preventing the main chain from becoming congested. Each sidechain can independently index and store data, process queries, and even perform algorithmic tasks, such as ranking results. Since sidechains operate independently, they can process transactions and queries in parallel, significantly improving the speed and scalability of the entire system.

For example, a decentralized search engine could be implemented such that each sidechain is responsible for a particular category of search data, such as news, images, or videos. As users submit queries, the main blockchain can coordinate the query processing by interacting with the relevant sidechains. This ensures that the search engine remains fast and responsive even as the number of users and the amount of data grows exponentially.

Improving Indexing Speed Using Crawlers

In a traditional search engine, indexing is a crucial step in building the search index, which is used to quickly retrieve relevant results during a query. Decentralized search engines rely on distributed crawlers to perform this task. A distributed crawling system involves multiple nodes working in parallel to crawl websites, collect data, and update the search index. By decentralizing the crawling process, the system can scale and crawl a much larger portion of the internet without overwhelming any single node.

Distributed crawlers can be incentivized to participate in the crawling process through the use of a token-based system, where nodes are rewarded for performing crawls. These crawlers can work asynchronously, each focusing on different sections of the web or specific categories of data. For example, one crawler may focus on news sites, while another might crawl e-commerce platforms. As the crawlers index data, they update the blockchain, which stores references to the indexed pages along with metadata. This decentralized approach allows for continuous and rapid indexing without requiring a centralized server to manage the task.

To improve indexing speed, crawlers can be optimized through various strategies, such as

Parallel processing Distributing the crawling task across many nodes to allow simultaneous crawling of multiple pages.

Efficient data structures Using optimized data structures such as Bloom filters or inverted indices to minimize the amount of data that needs to be processed and stored.

Prioritization Crawling more relevant or frequently updated websites first, ensuring that the search engine's index remains up-to-date with the latest content.

By scaling the crawling process using a distributed approach, the indexing speed of the search engine can be significantly improved, enabling faster search results and more comprehensive coverage of the web.

Caching and Data Replication

One of the critical factors affecting the performance of a decentralized search engine is the time it takes to retrieve data from the network. This latency can be especially problematic in a distributed system, where data may reside on nodes spread across multiple geographic locations. To mitigate this issue, caching and data replication techniques can be employed to reduce the time it takes to retrieve search results.

Caching involves storing frequently accessed data in memory or on a local disk, allowing it to be quickly retrieved without needing to perform a time-consuming search across the entire network. In a decentralized search engine, the query results can be cached at various levels at the local node level, within a specific sidechain, or even within the global network. By caching common queries or popular results, the system can avoid redundant searches, reducing latency and improving response times.

Data replication, on the other hand, involves creating copies of data and distributing them across multiple nodes in the network. By replicating data across different geographic regions or within specific nodes that handle high volumes of traffic, the system can reduce the time it takes to fetch results. Data replication ensures that copies of the indexed data are available closer to the user, allowing the search engine to deliver results quickly without the need for long-distance communication.

Together, caching and data replication can drastically reduce the time it takes to process a query, providing low-latency search experiences even in a decentralized environment.

Reducing Consensus Overhead Using Authority

In decentralized systems, consensus mechanisms are used to ensure that all participants agree on the current state of the system. However, consensus algorithms like Proof of Work (PoW) or Proof of Stake

(PoS) can introduce significant overhead, particularly in terms of computational resources and time. This overhead can hinder the performance of decentralized systems, especially when high throughput is required, such as in the case of search queries.

Proof of Authority (PoA) is a consensus mechanism that can reduce the overhead typically associated with PoW and PoS. In PoA, instead of relying on a large number of validators or miners to verify transactions, a small set of trusted authorities are selected to validate transactions. These authorities are usually pre-approved and hold reputations within the network. PoA does not require complex cryptographic puzzles or staking of tokens, which significantly reduces the time and computational resources needed to reach consensus.

In the context of a decentralized search engine, PoA can be used to validate and verify the indexing and querying processes more efficiently. Since PoA does not require a global consensus, the system can achieve faster transaction finality, reducing the time it takes to process search queries. Additionally, PoA reduces the computational load on nodes, allowing them to focus more on indexing and querying tasks rather than consensus participation.

Configurations Using IPFS and Ethereum

To illustrate how these performance tuning techniques can be implemented in a decentralized search engine, consider the following configuration using IPFS and Ethereum.

IPFS (InterPlanetary File System) IPFS can be used for storing and distributing the search engine's index in a decentralized manner. Each piece of data, such as indexed web pages or search results, is stored as a content-addressable object in the IPFS network. By using IPFS, the system ensures that the data is distributed across multiple nodes, providing redundancy and improving the scalability of the search engine.

Ethereum (or any blockchain with smart contract support) Ethereum can be used to store metadata about the indexed pages and handle the governance aspects of the search engine. Smart contracts on Ethereum can manage voting for algorithm updates, reward distribution for crawlers, and transaction logs for auditing purposes. The use of Ethereum's decentralized network allows for tamper-proof data storage and transparent algorithm updates.

Load Balancing with Sidechains To improve scalability, the system can use Ethereum sidechains to handle specific tasks like processing queries or indexing certain data types. By distributing the workload across different chains, the main Ethereum chain remains uncongested, and the system can process a large number of transactions concurrently.

Optimizing performance and scalability is crucial for the success of a decentralized search engine. Techniques such as sharding, load balancing using blockchain sidechains, distributed crawling, caching, and data replication ensure that the system remains fast and responsive, even as the number of users and data increases. Additionally, adopting consensus mechanisms like Proof of Authority reduces the overhead typically associated with more resource-intensive consensus models. By employing these strategies, a decentralized search engine can achieve high performance, low latency, and scalability, ensuring that it remains competitive with centralized systems while maintaining its decentralized nature.

Chapter 14

Building a Complete Decentralized Search Engine – A Step-by-Step Guide

Building a fully functional decentralized search engine from the ground up involves several layers of complexity, from setting up a robust backend to deploying decentralized data storage and integrating AI-based ranking algorithms. In this chapter, we will guide you through the essential steps involved in creating a decentralized search engine that can crawl, index, and rank search results autonomously using a blockchain-based infrastructure. The goal is to create a decentralized, scalable, and efficient search system that is capable of delivering accurate and relevant search results, all while ensuring the privacy of users and providing transparency through blockchain technology.

Setting Up the Backend Using Django

Before we dive into the decentralized components of the search engine, it's essential to have a solid backend structure in place to handle core functionalities such as user interactions, query processing, and the integration of the blockchain components. For this, we will use Django or Flask, two of the most popular Python web frameworks. Both Django and Flask are well-suited for building the backend of a decentralized search engine, but the choice of which framework to use will depend on your specific needs.

Django is a full-stack framework that includes everything you need to build a web application, such as an ORM (Object-Relational Mapping) system, routing, authentication, and more. If you need a complete, opinionated framework with built-in functionalities for handling databases, APIs, and user management, Django is a great choice.

Flask, on the other hand, is a micro-framework that gives you more flexibility by leaving many decisions up to the developer. Flask is lightweight and well-suited for small applications or projects where you want more control over the components you integrate.

In this step-by-step guide, we will assume you're using **Django**, as it provides a more comprehensive toolset for building a web application quickly. However, you can easily adapt the instructions if you're using Flask.

Install Django To get started with Django, first, you need to install the framework. You can do this by running the following command in your terminal

    pip install django

Create a New Django Project Once Django is installed, create a new project by running

    django-admin startproject decentralized_search

This will create a new project folder with the necessary files for your Django application.

Set Up Database Django uses an SQL database by default. However, since we are building a decentralized search engine, we will be using IPFS for data storage. You will still need a database to manage user queries, preferences, and metadata related to search results. You can choose between SQLite, PostgreSQL, or MySQL as your database backend.

Create the Search Application Inside your Django project, you can create an application specifically for handling search functionality by running

```
python manage.py startapp search
```

This will create a new folder for the search application, where you will implement the core search functionality, user queries, and ranking algorithms.

Building a Decentralized Index Using IPFS

With the backend in place, the next step is to create a decentralized index for your search engine. Traditional search engines use centralized databases to store indexed content, but in a decentralized search engine, the data must be stored across multiple nodes using a decentralized file system like IPFS (InterPlanetary File System).

IPFS is a protocol and network designed to create peer-to-peer distributed file systems. It allows for the creation of an immutable and distributed data storage system, making it an ideal choice for a decentralized search engine.

To build the decentralized index, we will use **IPFS** to store the search results, indexed web pages, and metadata in a distributed manner. When a new webpage is indexed, the content is split into small chunks, and each chunk is assigned a unique cryptographic hash. These chunks are then stored across different nodes in the IPFS network. When a user queries the search engine, the engine retrieves the relevant content from IPFS based on the associated hashes.

Steps to Integrate IPFS

Install IPFS To start using IPFS, you need to install the IPFS daemon. You can download the IPFS software from the official website or install it via package managers like apt or brew.

```
ipfs init
ipfs daemon
```

Integrate IPFS with Django To interact with IPFS from within your Django application, you can use a

Python library such as ipfshttpclient. Install it by running

pip install ipfshttpclient

You can then use this library to add files to IPFS, retrieve files, and manage the decentralized index.

Indexing Web Pages When a webpage is crawled, the content is uploaded to IPFS. You can generate a hash for the content and store it in your database, linking it to the corresponding query results. This ensures that the content is easily retrievable and can be served quickly.

Integrating an AI-Based Ranking Algorithm

A critical component of any search engine is the ranking algorithm, which determines the relevance of search results based on the user's query. In a decentralized search engine, the ranking algorithm needs to be efficient and capable of working with distributed data sources while ensuring that the results returned are both relevant and accurate.

In this section, we will integrate an **AI-based ranking algorithm** using machine learning techniques. The ranking system will use features such as keyword matching, user feedback, and the content's popularity to determine the most relevant results for a given query.

We can implement an AI-based ranking algorithm using **TensorFlow** or **Keras**, which are popular libraries for building machine learning models. The algorithm will use a deep learning model trained on a large dataset of web pages and search queries.

Steps to Implement the Ranking Algorithm

Data Collection Collect a dataset of web pages and queries to train the machine learning model. This dataset should contain pairs of search queries and the relevant web pages that were retrieved for those queries.

Feature Extraction Extract features such as keyword frequency, semantic similarity, and content relevance from the web pages to train the model. You can use techniques like TF-IDF (Term Frequency-Inverse Document Frequency) or word embeddings like Word2Vec to transform the content into a format that the model can process.

Train the Model Use the extracted features to train the deep learning model. The model will learn to predict the relevance of a web page for a given query. The model can be trained using a feed-forward neural network or more advanced architectures like recurrent neural networks (RNNs) or transformers.

Integrate the Model into the Backend Once the model is trained, you can integrate it into your Django application, where it will process incoming search queries and rank the results accordingly. The model can be served via an API endpoint that the backend can call to retrieve ranked results.

Deploying Smart Contracts on Ethereum

To ensure transparency, fairness, and decentralization, we will deploy **smart contracts** on the **Ethereum blockchain**. These smart contracts will handle various functions such as

Incentivizing crawlers and indexers Smart contracts will reward nodes that participate in crawling and indexing web pages.

Governance Smart contracts will allow token holders to vote on algorithm updates and other governance decisions.

To deploy the smart contracts on Ethereum, we will use **Solidity**, the most widely used programming language for writing smart contracts.

Steps to Deploy Smart Contracts

Set Up Ethereum Development Environment
Install **Truffle** or **Hardhat**, which are frameworks that simplify the development, testing, and deployment of smart contracts. You will also need a **MetaMask** wallet to interact with the Ethereum network.

Write the Smart Contracts In Solidity, write smart contracts to define how the tokens will be distributed, how governance will work, and how crawling rewards will be handled. For example, a simple contract for rewarding crawlers could look like this

```
pragma solidity ^0.8.0;

contract SearchEngine {
    mapping(address => uint256) public rewards;

    function rewardCrawler(address crawler) public {
        rewards[crawler] += 1;
    }

    function withdrawRewards() public {
        uint256 amount = rewards[msg.sender];
        rewards[msg.sender] = 0;
        payable(msg.sender).transfer(amount);
    }
}
```

Deploy the Smart Contracts After writing and testing the smart contracts, deploy them to the

Ethereum network using Truffle or Hardhat. You will need to interact with the Ethereum network through a testnet (e.g., Rinkeby or Kovan) before deploying to the mainnet.

Integrate Smart Contracts with Django Use web3.py, a Python library for interacting with Ethereum, to call the smart contracts from your Django application. You can use web3.py to send transactions, check balances, and retrieve rewards information.

Source Code, Deployment Instructions

Once all components have been developed, you can compile the complete source code for your decentralized search engine. This will include

Django Backend Code for handling user queries, integrating with IPFS, and serving ranked search results.

IPFS Integration to store and retrieve data from the decentralized network.

Machine Learning Code for training and serving the ranking model.

Solidity Smart Contracts for incentivizing crawlers, managing token rewards, and enabling governance.

To ensure the system is working as expected, you can create a series of **test scenarios** that cover different aspects of the search engine,

Chapter 15

Case Studies and Real-World Applications

In this chapter, we will delve into several notable decentralized search engine projects, each with its own unique approach to achieving decentralization, user privacy, and governance. These case studies will provide practical insights into the advantages and challenges of building decentralized search engines. We will also explore the technical aspects of these projects, offering a comparative analysis of their approaches, features, and impact on the broader landscape of online search.

Presearch and Its Token-Based Model

Presearch is one of the most well-known decentralized search engines that integrates blockchain technology with search. The core idea behind Presearch is to empower users by allowing them to participate in the search process, while also rewarding them for their activity. The Presearch network uses a **token-based model** where users are rewarded with **PRE tokens** for performing searches on the platform. These tokens can be used to pay for ads, participate in governance, or exchanged on cryptocurrency exchanges.

Presearch operates with a unique advantage it is built on a blockchain that enables **decentralized indexing** and **search result rankings**. Unlike traditional search engines, which rely on proprietary algorithms to index and rank content, Presearch distributes the indexing and ranking processes across a network of nodes. These nodes are incentivized with PRE tokens, creating a **decentralized incentive structure** that encourages participants to contribute their resources.

In terms of architecture, Presearch uses a **proof-of-stake (PoS)** consensus mechanism to verify and validate the content and search results. This provides a high level of transparency, ensuring that all search queries are processed in a way that is verifiable and not controlled by a single entity. Moreover, the use of blockchain technology ensures that search data remains **private** and **non-tracked**, which aligns with growing concerns about online privacy.

The **Presearch API** allows developers to integrate decentralized search into their applications, and through this mechanism, Presearch has attracted a community of developers and users who benefit from more transparent and privacy-focused search services. Presearch is an excellent example of a decentralized search engine that utilizes blockchain technology to give users control over their data, while also incorporating a reward system that incentivizes active participation.

Lessons Learned from Presearch While Presearch has made notable strides in promoting decentralization in search, the platform faces challenges in scaling and delivering competitive search results on par with centralized giants like Google. Its token-based model has also encountered criticisms regarding the market value and sustainability of PRE tokens. The project also needs to address issues related to content moderation and quality control, as decentralization often leads to fragmented and inconsistent search results. These are important lessons to consider when building a decentralized search engine balancing decentralization with effective content moderation and ensuring the long-term value of reward mechanisms are critical to success.

SearX and Federated Search Models

SearX is another pioneering decentralized search engine that focuses on **federated search**. Unlike Presearch, which relies on a fully decentralized blockchain infrastructure, SearX is built on the concept of **meta-search**. It aggregates search results from multiple sources, such as Google, Bing, DuckDuckGo, and other search engines, without tracking user activity or storing personal data. This federated approach allows SearX to bypass centralized control, providing users with search results from a variety of sources while maintaining privacy.

The platform's **open-source nature** is a critical factor in its success, allowing anyone to set up their own instance of SearX. By doing so, users are not limited to a single search engine and are not subject to the algorithms or biases imposed by centralized search platforms. Each SearX instance is independent, but they all communicate with each other, sharing the same underlying open-source code.

SearX supports multiple **search categories** like web search, image search, video search, and more, all while maintaining the privacy and anonymity of users. The search queries are sent to multiple search engines and aggregate results are displayed to the user without logging or tracking any personal information. The federated search model helps to decentralize the data retrieval process, although the underlying search engines (such as Google or Bing) may still be centralized.

SearX's privacy-first approach is enhanced by using encrypted connections and minimizing data retention. The platform doesn't collect any identifiable user data, making it a viable option for those concerned with data privacy. Users also have the ability to **self-host** their own instance of SearX, thus enhancing decentralization and allowing anyone to contribute to the project by hosting an instance and making it available to others.

Lessons Learned from SearX SearX's federated model highlights the importance of user privacy and freedom from centralized control, but it also demonstrates the limitations of aggregating content from centralized sources. Since SearX relies on third-party search engines, its ability to provide fully decentralized results is limited, especially in terms of ranking and indexing. Additionally, the reliance on multiple sources for search data can lead to slower response times, particularly when aggregating results from a variety of engines.

While SearX does not control the search content itself, it has proven to be an excellent solution for users who are primarily concerned with privacy and avoiding data tracking. It serves as a good example of how **federated search** can enhance privacy but also requires cooperation and collaboration between different nodes to function effectively.

Brave and Private Search Integration

Brave is a privacy-focused web browser that has integrated a **decentralized search engine** into its platform. Unlike traditional browsers, Brave blocks trackers and ads by default, offering users a more private and secure browsing experience. One of the significant developments for Brave is the introduction of its own **Brave Search** engine, which aims to provide an alternative to search engines like Google while preserving privacy.

Brave Search is built on an independent, **decentralized index**, separate from other search engines, and uses **privacy-preserving techniques** such as **on-device search processing** to ensure that users' data is never stored or tracked. The Brave browser integrates with the search engine, ensuring that search queries remain anonymous, and results are not influenced by user data, cookies, or browsing history.

Another important feature of Brave Search is its integration with the **Basic Attention Token (BAT)**, a cryptocurrency that rewards users for their engagement with ads and content. Brave's model is based on incentivizing users while ensuring that their privacy is maintained. Users can choose to participate in the BAT system and earn rewards for opting into ads. This aligns with the broader goals of **decentralization**, as Brave aims to remove third-party ad networks and bring more control to users over their data.

Brave's decentralized search engine further pushes the envelope of privacy and transparency by offering search results that are **unbiased** and **unfiltered** by corporate interests, a significant advantage over traditional search engines that manipulate results for profit.

Lessons Learned from Brave Brave's success shows that privacy and decentralization are valuable features that users are increasingly looking for. However, the challenge lies in providing competitive search results while maintaining privacy. The Brave Search engine is still in development, and while it's gaining traction, it faces stiff competition from established players like Google and Bing. It also faces challenges in terms of user adoption, as many people are reluctant to switch from familiar, mainstream search engines.

Brave's integration of **cryptocurrency** rewards offers a new model of user incentives but requires critical mass for it to work sustainably. For a decentralized search engine to be truly successful, it must offer a **high-quality user experience** while ensuring that privacy and decentralization do not come at the cost of usability or search accuracy.

Challenges and Lessons from These Projects

Each of the decentralized search projects discussed— Presearch, SearX, and Brave—has made strides in offering alternatives to traditional, centralized search engines. However, all of these projects face challenges in terms of scalability, performance, user adoption, and search result quality.

One of the most significant challenges is **ensuring the quality of search results** while maintaining decentralization. Traditional search engines rely heavily on advanced ranking algorithms, vast amounts of data, and machine learning models to deliver the most relevant search results. Replicating this capability in a decentralized network while ensuring that the process remains transparent and privacy-centric is no easy feat. Decentralized search engines also face issues such as **indexing speed**, **data consistency**, and **load balancing** in a distributed environment.

Moreover, the issue of **incentivization** remains critical. While models like Presearch's token system and Brave's BAT provide interesting solutions, these models need to be carefully calibrated to ensure they are both sustainable and valuable to the user base. A decentralized search engine must also establish **strong governance models** to ensure that the system remains fair, transparent, and free from manipulation.

Despite these challenges, the efforts made by these projects demonstrate that decentralization in search is not only feasible but also necessary to create a more **open, transparent, and user-centric** web. By focusing on privacy, incentivization, and transparency, these projects provide a glimpse into the future of search and how it can be reshaped using blockchain and decentralized technologies.

Comparative Analysis

Feature	Presearch	SearX	Brave Search
Decentralization	High (token-based rewards, distributed indexing)	Moderate (federated model)	High (independent decentralized index)
Privacy	High (anonymous searches, token rewards)	High (no user tracking)	High (on-device search processing, no tracking)
User Incentives	PRE tokens for search activity	None	BAT tokens for ad engagement
Search Results	Aggregated, decentralized ranking	Aggregated from multiple search engines	Independent, privacy-focused results
Governance	Token-based	Open-	Centralized

Feature	Presearch	SearX	Brave Search
	(community voting)	source, community-driven	governance with decentralized indexing
Scalability	Moderate (blockchain reliance)	High (federated, self-hosted)	

Chapter 16

Future of Decentralized Search and AI Integration

The future of decentralized search and artificial intelligence (AI) is poised to transform the way information is accessed, processed, and delivered. As technological advancements continue to accelerate, decentralized search engines will increasingly integrate cutting-edge AI models, quantum computing capabilities, and cross-chain interoperability to create more efficient, secure, and intelligent search platforms. This chapter explores the key trends that will define the future of decentralized search and AI, including the role of quantum computing, the emergence of self-learning AI models for search optimization, the potential for cross-chain interoperability, and the ethical implications of AI and decentralization. The objective is to provide readers with a comprehensive understanding of how these technologies will shape the future of search, offering both technical insights and strategic perspectives on innovative directions in search technology.

Quantum Computing

Quantum computing is expected to revolutionize the search landscape by dramatically increasing the processing power available for indexing, querying, and ranking search results. Traditional search engines rely on classical binary-based computing, where data is processed in terms of bits (0 or 1). In contrast, quantum computing leverages quantum bits or qubits, which can exist in multiple states simultaneously due to the principles of superposition and entanglement.

The exponential increase in computational power offered by quantum computers will have profound implications for search algorithms. A classical search engine processes search queries sequentially or in parallel across a finite number of servers. Quantum computers, however, will be able to process all possible search query combinations simultaneously, reducing search times from minutes or seconds to milliseconds. Grover's algorithm, a quantum search algorithm, has already demonstrated the potential to search unsorted data with quadratic speedup compared to classical algorithms.

Impact on Indexing and Ranking

Quantum computing will enable real-time indexing of vast amounts of data, including dynamic content such as social media posts, live videos, and constantly updated news feeds. Traditional search engines often rely on scheduled crawls and indexing, which introduce latency between content publication and search availability. Quantum-enhanced search engines could eliminate this delay by continuously indexing content as it is created. Furthermore, quantum-based ranking algorithms will optimize relevance and personalization by rapidly analyzing complex user behavior patterns and semantic relationships between data points.

Improved Encryption and Security

Decentralized search engines rely on cryptographic techniques to protect user privacy and data integrity. Quantum computing poses a dual threat and opportunity in this area. While quantum computers have the potential to break existing encryption algorithms, they can also be used to develop new quantum-resistant encryption techniques, such as lattice-based and post-quantum cryptography, ensuring the continued security of decentralized search networks.

The table below compares the capabilities of classical search and quantum-enhanced search engines

Feature	Classical Search Engines	Quantum-Enhanced Search Engines
Indexing Speed	Limited by sequential processing	Real-time indexing using parallel quantum states
Search Time	Linear or logarithmic scaling	Quadratic or exponential speedup

Feature	Classical Search Engines	Quantum-Enhanced Search Engines
Personalization	Based on limited behavioral data	Enhanced by multi-dimensional behavioral analysis
Security	Vulnerable to quantum decryption	Strengthened by quantum-resistant cryptography

Self-Learning AI Models

Self-learning AI models represent a significant advancement in search technology, enabling search engines to continuously improve their performance based on user interactions and feedback. Traditional search engines rely on manually defined ranking factors, such as keyword density, backlinks, and domain authority. In contrast, self-learning AI models use reinforcement learning, deep learning, and natural language processing (NLP) to adapt and refine search algorithms automatically.

Reinforcement Learning for Search Optimization

Reinforcement learning allows AI models to optimize search results by learning from user behavior. When a user clicks on a search result and spends significant

168

time on the page, the model interprets this as a positive signal, reinforcing the ranking of similar content. Conversely, if a user quickly returns to the search results page, the model recognizes this as a negative signal and adjusts future rankings accordingly.

Semantic Search and Context Awareness

Self-learning AI models enhance search accuracy by understanding the context and intent behind search queries. For example, a search for "apple" could refer to the fruit, the technology company, or a specific product. NLP models such as BERT (Bidirectional Encoder Representations from Transformers) and GPT (Generative Pre-trained Transformer) enable search engines to interpret the contextual meaning of queries and provide more relevant results.

AI-Based Content Categorization

Self-learning models improve the categorization and clustering of search results by identifying patterns and relationships between different content types. This enables decentralized search engines to present more structured and organized results, enhancing the user experience.

The diagram below illustrates the process of AI-based search optimization

The table below outlines the differences between traditional and AI-driven search engines

Feature	Traditional Search Engines	AI-Driven Search Engines
Learning Mechanism	Manual tuning of ranking factors	Self-learning and adaptation
Context Recognition	Keyword-based matching	Contextual and semantic understanding
Result Quality	Static and	Dynamic and

Feature	Traditional Search Engines	AI-Driven Search Engines
	predictable	personalized
Feedback Integration	Limited user feedback	Real-time learning from user behavior

Cross-Chain Interoperability

Decentralized search engines are typically built on specific blockchain networks, such as Ethereum, Polkadot, or Solana. Each of these networks operates independently, creating barriers to data exchange and cross-platform search functionality. Cross-chain interoperability allows decentralized search engines to access and index data from multiple blockchain networks, enhancing the depth and breadth of search results.

Interoperability via Bridge Protocols

Bridge protocols enable data transfer between different blockchain networks. For example, the Polkadot network uses parachains to facilitate cross-chain communication, allowing decentralized search engines to aggregate data from diverse sources. Cross-chain interoperability ensures that search engines are not

restricted to data within a single blockchain
ecosystem.

Unified Search Index

By combining data from multiple blockchains,
decentralized search engines can create a unified
search index, improving the comprehensiveness and
accuracy of search results. This enables users to
search for NFTs, smart contracts, and decentralized
applications (DApps) across different networks using a
single interface.

Challenges and Solutions

Cross-chain search introduces challenges such as
data format inconsistencies, varying consensus
mechanisms, and network latency. Standardized data
formats and consensus protocols, such as the
Interledger Protocol (ILP) and Cross-Chain
Communication Protocol (CCP), are being developed to
address these issues.

Ethical Implications of AI

The integration of AI and decentralization raises
important ethical questions regarding privacy, bias,
and control over information.

Data Privacy and Ownership

Decentralized search engines empower users to retain control over their search history and personal data. However, the use of AI models for personalization requires access to user behavior data, creating a tension between privacy and performance. Privacy-preserving techniques such as federated learning and homomorphic encryption can help balance these competing interests.

Algorithmic Bias and Fairness

AI-driven search engines are vulnerable to bias introduced during model training. If the training data reflects social or political biases, the search engine may inadvertently reinforce these biases. Decentralized governance models, where users have voting rights over algorithm updates, can help mitigate this risk.

Transparency and Accountability

Decentralized search engines must maintain transparency in how search algorithms operate and rank content. Open-source models and decentralized auditing mechanisms ensure that search engines remain accountable to their user base.

The future of decentralized search will be shaped by quantum computing, self-learning AI models, cross-chain interoperability, and evolving ethical standards. Quantum computing will revolutionize search speed and complexity, self-learning AI models will enhance relevance and personalization, cross-chain interoperability will unify data from multiple blockchains, and ethical frameworks will ensure user trust and fairness. By understanding these emerging trends, readers will be well-positioned to contribute to and benefit from the next generation of search technology.

The evolution of decentralized search engines represents a significant shift in the way information is accessed, processed, and controlled. Over the course of this book, the fundamental concepts, technologies, and challenges involved in building and operating a decentralized search engine have been explored in depth. From the architectural design and indexing strategies to the integration of artificial intelligence (AI) and blockchain technology, readers have gained a comprehensive understanding of how decentralized search works and how it is poised to reshape the future of information retrieval. This conclusion will summarize the key takeaways from the book, provide practical advice for those interested in building their own decentralized search engine, and reflect on the growing importance of AI and blockchain in the future of search technology.

Decentralized search engines offer a revolutionary alternative to traditional search platforms by eliminating the need for centralized control, improving privacy, and enhancing transparency. Traditional search engines like Google and Bing rely on proprietary algorithms and centralized data storage, giving them significant control over the flow of information and user data. This centralization raises concerns about censorship, privacy violations, and algorithmic manipulation. In contrast, decentralized search engines distribute indexing, ranking, and search functions across a blockchain-based network, removing single points of control and enhancing user autonomy.

One of the core takeaways from this book is the importance of decentralization in restoring user privacy and control over personal data. Decentralized search engines enable users to retain ownership of their search history and preferences without relying on third-party platforms to store and manage this information. Through the use of cryptographic techniques and blockchain-based consensus mechanisms, decentralized search engines ensure that data remains secure and verifiable while minimizing the risk of tampering or unauthorized access.

AI integration has emerged as a transformative force in improving the performance and relevance of decentralized search. Traditional keyword-based search models are limited in their ability to understand user intent and context. AI-driven models, including natural language processing (NLP) and deep learning, have introduced semantic search capabilities that enable decentralized search engines to deliver more accurate and personalized results. AI models can analyze user behavior, identify patterns, and continuously adapt search algorithms to improve relevance and accuracy over time. Reinforcement learning, transfer learning, and federated learning techniques have further enhanced the adaptability and intelligence of decentralized search platforms.

The importance of cross-chain interoperability in decentralized search cannot be overstated. Blockchain-based search engines are often confined to individual networks, such as Ethereum, Polkadot, or Solana, limiting their ability to index and retrieve data across multiple ecosystems. Cross-chain communication protocols and bridge technologies have enabled decentralized search engines to aggregate and index data from different blockchains, creating a unified search experience. The development of Interledger Protocol (ILP) and Cross-Chain Communication Protocol (CCP) has played a crucial role in breaking down these barriers and enabling seamless data exchange between different blockchain networks.

From a technical perspective, building a decentralized search engine requires a deep understanding of blockchain architecture, consensus mechanisms, data indexing, and AI-based search optimization. The implementation of a peer-to-peer network for data distribution, combined with a token-based incentive system to reward contributors and validators, forms the backbone of most decentralized search platforms. Effective indexing strategies, including inverted indexes and vector-based search models, are critical to ensuring fast and accurate query processing. The integration of AI for contextual understanding, ranking, and semantic analysis further enhances the user experience and ensures that search results are relevant and meaningful.

Building a Decentralized Search Engine

For readers interested in building their own decentralized search engine, it is essential to approach the project with a clear understanding of the technical, operational, and strategic challenges involved. The first step is to define the scope and purpose of the search engine. Unlike traditional search engines that aim to index the entire internet, decentralized search engines often focus on niche markets or specific types of content, such as decentralized applications (DApps), non-fungible tokens (NFTs), or smart contracts. By focusing on a well-defined content domain, developers can streamline the indexing process and improve the relevance of search results.

The choice of blockchain infrastructure is a critical factor in the design of a decentralized search engine. Ethereum, Polkadot, and Solana offer different trade-offs in terms of scalability, transaction costs, and smart contract functionality. Developers must evaluate these factors based on the expected search volume, the complexity of search queries, and the need for real-time indexing and retrieval. Implementing a scalable peer-to-peer network architecture ensures that data is distributed efficiently across the network, reducing latency and improving search performance.

Effective indexing is one of the most challenging aspects of decentralized search. Traditional search engines use centralized server farms to build and maintain complex search indexes. Decentralized search engines, by contrast, rely on distributed indexing strategies, where data is fragmented and stored across multiple nodes. Inverted indexing, vector-based search models, and semantic search techniques can help improve indexing efficiency and query response times. Developers should also consider using decentralized file storage systems, such as the

InterPlanetary File System (IPFS), to store and retrieve indexed data securely.

AI-driven search optimization is another key consideration when building a decentralized search engine. Machine learning models can be used to analyze user behavior, identify patterns, and refine search algorithms over time. Reinforcement learning, where the search engine continuously adapts based on user feedback, can help improve the ranking and relevance of search results. Transfer learning, where pre-trained AI models are adapted to new search domains, can further accelerate the development process. The use of NLP models, such as BERT and GPT, enables the search engine to understand user intent and deliver more accurate and context-aware results.

The implementation of a token-based incentive model is essential for ensuring the sustainability and scalability of a decentralized search engine. Users, validators, and data contributors should be rewarded with native tokens for their participation and contributions to the network. Governance models, including decentralized autonomous organizations (DAOs), can be used to enable community-based decision-making and ensure that the search engine evolves in line with user needs and preferences.

The Growing Importance of Blockchain

AI and blockchain technology are set to play an increasingly important role in the future of search. AI has already demonstrated its ability to improve search accuracy and relevance through semantic search, intent recognition, and personalization. As AI models become more sophisticated and capable of processing larger datasets, the performance of decentralized search engines will continue to improve. AI-powered ranking algorithms will enable search engines to deliver more meaningful and targeted search results, reducing information overload and improving user satisfaction.

Blockchain technology offers a unique solution to the challenges of privacy, censorship, and centralization in search. By decentralizing data storage and search functions, blockchain-based search engines eliminate single points of failure and enhance data integrity and security. Blockchain-based consensus mechanisms, such as proof of stake (PoS) and proof of work (PoW), ensure that search engines operate in a trustless and transparent manner. Smart contracts enable the automation of key search functions, including indexing, ranking, and query processing, further improving the efficiency and scalability of decentralized search engines.

The convergence of AI and blockchain in search technology represents a paradigm shift in information retrieval. AI provides the intelligence needed to understand and rank complex search queries, while blockchain ensures the transparency and security of search operations. Cross-chain interoperability further enhances the depth and breadth of search results, enabling users to access information from multiple blockchain ecosystems through a single interface. The integration of quantum computing, self-learning AI models, and decentralized governance structures will further accelerate the evolution of search technology in the coming years.

Building a decentralized search engine is a complex but rewarding endeavor. The knowledge gained from this book will equip readers with the technical expertise and strategic insights needed to design, develop, and deploy a decentralized search platform. As the demand for privacy, transparency, and user control continues to grow, decentralized search engines will play an increasingly important role in shaping the future of information access. Readers are encouraged to explore innovative approaches, experiment with new AI and blockchain-based solutions, and contribute to the development of decentralized search technology. By combining technical expertise with a forward-thinking mindset, readers can position themselves at the forefront of this exciting technological revolution.

THE END